ALL NEW
Government
SECRETS

★ ★ ★ ★ ★ ★

Nancy S. Garascia
Nick Isenberg
Phyllis Schomaker

Publications International, Ltd.

Nancy S. Garaşcia is a freelance writer based in Barrington, Illinois. She is the author of four books, including *Ancestor Hunt: Finding Your Family Online,* a forthcoming book for teens. She also teaches nonfiction writing online for UCLA Extension.

Nick Isenberg is a freelance reporter based in Glenwood Springs, Colorado, who specializes in empowerment articles. His credits range from *The Washington Post* to *The National Enquirer* and include CNN, CBS, and many public radio programs.

Phyllis Schomaker is a freelance writer and researcher who lives and works in Jefferson City, Missouri. She has written several books on home and consumer issues and has built a decade-long career in library and information science. Government research is one of her specialties.

FedEx is a registered trademark of FedEx Corporation. NetPost is a trademark of the United States Postal Service.

CONTENTS

★ ★ ★ ★

Revealing New Secrets for a New Era

* * * *

I SEEMS OBVIOUS that the government would keep secrets. We all have a thing or two we'd like to keep to ourselves, and why should the government be any different?

It starts to get tricky, however, when government officials decide what should be kept secret and what should not. Some information, such as wartime intelligence, is kept secret for good reasons, but other information may just protect an official from being embarrassed. And some information is secret because we just haven't been paying attention—it's widely available, but no one has bothered to look for it.

All New Government Secrets takes a look at government to find out what you should know. You will read about various kinds of secrets—some important information concerning taxes and Social Security and other less important, though quite interesting, curiosities.

You will read about where your tax dollars go, but you'll also find out about a few ways to recapture those dollars in government programs and giveaways. Would you like to buy some cheap wilderness acreage? That information is here. Do you already have land that you'd like to turn into a government-sponsored wetland? You'll learn about that, too.

Another way government keeps secrets is through confusing legalistic language. Sometimes you can read every word on a government document and still have no idea what it means. *All New Government Secrets* sidesteps that problem, however, with the simple solution of crisp, clear language. You'll get straight talk on the 2001 tax reform law and what it can mean for you. If you're a senior citizen, then you're used to dealing with Social Security and Medicare, and you know how frustrating that can be. Don't worry—*All New Government Secrets* includes some tips to make your life easier, as well.

There may be no group that deserves our thanks and respect as much as our veterans, whether they be young or old. It's not a secret that the government provides a number of programs for veterans, but sometimes the details of those programs are so little known and understood that they might as well be secret. Statistics show that only 11 percent of surviving vets from World War I, World War II, and the Korean Conflict are cashing in on their benefits, even including pensions. If you're a vet, this book has some pointers to make sure you receive everything you've earned in your service to your country.

Not all secrets are negative. The government has some helpful, positive secrets, too. Would you like to get some money from the government just for being creative? This book will tell you how. If you're a teacher or a police officer, would you like to buy a home for half price? You can read all the details here. Have you ever had difficulty with Customs when crossing the border? You'll learn ways to avoid it.

The United States is an open society. We have free access to information and many government secrets. But it never hurts to have a little help in looking.

GOODIES FROM UNCLE SAM

★ ★ ★

EVERYBODY HATES paying taxes. But it's much less painful if you can find a way to put some of that tax money back into your own pocket. Government programs that offer cash to taxpayers are constantly being created, but most people don't know they exist. Your tax dollars are also used to fund programs that protect or increase the value of your home and that give you services for free or at a reasonable cost. Here are some ways you can jump on the government gravy train.

MONEY FOR CREATIVITY

The government funds an incredible amount of artistic activity—such as film festivals, poetry in the schools, and symphony orchestras—through the National Endowment for the Arts (NEA). If you belong to an arts group, thousands of dollars could be yours.

The NEA also funds a small number of individual writers in poetry, fiction, creative nonfiction, and translation. If your work has significant artistic merit, you could be awarded as much as $20,000 per year, renewable for two years. Grants for the presentation, documentation, and preservation of the work of "master folk artists" are also made through the National Heritage Awards in the Folk & Traditional Arts. You can find information, guidelines, and applications for each of these programs at www.nea.gov.

SEE BEARS (AND BATTLEFIELDS AND CONCERTS) FOR FREE

The National Park Service has volunteer opportunities in many of its parks year-round. Some of them even pay a small stipend and provide housing or free camper hook-ups. "Volunteers-in-Parks" positions are available all over the country, from Acadia National Park in Maine to Yosemite National Park in California... and everywhere in between. For history buffs, there are openings at places like the Statue of Liberty, Mount Rushmore, and Ford's Theatre National Historic Site in Washington, D.C., where Lincoln was shot. Music lovers might want to volunteer to usher at Wolf Trap Farm Park for the Performing Arts or the New Orleans Jazz National Historical Park. Or maybe you just want to contemplate the natural beauty of Grand Canyon National Park, Isle Royale National Park in Michigan, or Padre Island National Seashore. More than 100 job listings, organized by park, can be viewed at www.nps.gov/volunteer, or you can call the National Park Service at 202-208-6843.

WHERE THE WILD THINGS ARE

The government has just made getting away from it all a little easier. Now you can search all federal lands for the perfect vacation spot using a special Web site: www.recreation.gov. You can search the site by keyword, state, or the type of activity you are pining for—like fishing, biking, boating, or hiking. You can also make sure you can bring your pet or RV. It can't get much easier than this.

LAND FOR SALE

Millions of acres of land out West belong to the American taxpayers, mostly in the form of parks and wildlife preserves. But sometimes the government decides it doesn't want a parcel of land anymore because it's standing in the way of community development and economic expansion, or it's just too isolated to manage properly. As a result, the Bureau of Land Management (BLM) offers some of these properties, located primarily in the western United States and Alaska, for public auction from time to time. The acreage isn't free, but for the right buyer it can be a terrific bargain. Here are the facts:

- Bids must reach a certain minimum, typically the appraised value of the land in comparison to surrounding properties.

- There is no set cost for any parcel.

- You are not required to attend the sale.

- You may submit a sealed bid or bid by phone.

To find out what bundles of land are currently up for auction, contact the BLM office in the state where you want to buy, or call the BLM at 202-452-5125. You can find contact information for BLM state offices at www.blm.gov/nhp/directory/index.htm.

IMPROVE YOUR HOME

You might be surprised to find you qualify for government grants of $1,000 or more to improve or repair your home. The Home Investment Partnerships Program (HOME) of the U.S. Department of Housing and Urban Development (HUD), offers these grants to homeowners whose income is no more than 80 percent of the median income in their area. In some expensive parts of the country, that can be an income of more than $40,000 per year for a couple.

HOME grants may be used for any "non-luxury" home improvements that do not raise the home's value to higher than 95 percent of the local median. Grants are most often given for modifications that enhance a home's accessibility, such as wheelchair ramps and shower grab bars, or for badly needed repairs, such as replacement of leaky roofs. For more information about whether you qualify for a HOME grant, contact your local HUD office. Consult the government pages of your telephone book or search the HUD office locator page at www.hud.gov/local/index.cfm. You may also write to: U.S. Department of Housing and Urban Development, 451 7th Street SW, Washington, D.C. 20410.

If you don't qualify for a HUD home improvement grant, for whatever reason, your bank may offer you a reverse mortgage. Don't take it. Sure, these loans do not require monthly payments and are paid back only when you sell your home or pass away.

However, they often carry higher interest rates than conventional home equity loans. And here's the real secret: If you have a lot of equity in your home and a long-term relationship with your bank, you should be able to negotiate a home-equity loan deal where you pay the lowest possible rate: the "prime" interest rate banks charge their best loan customers. Insist on it.

IMPROVE YOUR NEIGHBORHOOD

Uncle Sam wants to help you improve the community where you live. The most cost-effective way to do that is with a Section 203(k) rehabilitation loan, offered by the Federal Housing Authority (FHA) through banks and other lending institutions. Owners who want to repair or modernize a one- to four-family building that is at least one year old can avoid the high interest rates and short payback periods normally associated with construction loans. Instead, this loan combines both the mortgage to purchase the property and the funds to rehab it into one long-term mortgage. Any FHA-approved lender can give you the facts about this program, or on the Web you can take a look at www.hud.gov/fha/sfh/203k/203kabou.html.

HALF-PRICE HOMES FOR POLICE AND TEACHERS

Officials at HUD have re-launched their efforts to make housing more affordable for those who serve urban communities. Called Officer Next Door and Teacher Next Door, these two plans give police and teachers a 50-percent discount on HUD-owned single-family homes in "distressed" areas. Home buyers must simply be full-time police officers or teachers and agree to live in the houses for three years. More than 6,000 families have found low-cost housing through this program since 1997. For more information contact HUD at 202-708-1420, or go to www.hud.gov/buying/index.cfm for links to their Web pages.

SAVE MONEY ON ENERGY

The government *wants* you to save money on fuel costs. Insulation, high-efficiency heating and cooling systems, and energy-efficient windows can lower your utility bills by up to 50 percent. If you own your own home or are buying a home, you can finance some energy-friendly improvements through a wide variety of government-insured "energy-efficient

TOP SECRET

If you know someone who's poor, make sure they know about the government's Low Income Energy Assistance Program, a federally funded program that can help them meet their home heating and cooling needs. Find out where to apply at www.acf.dhhs.gov/programs/liheap/states.htm.

IDEAS FOR SAVING ENERGY

You can find many creative ways to lower your utility bills at the U.S. Department of Energy's Energy Efficiency and Renewable Energy Network (EREN) Web site, www.eren.doe.gov/consumerinfo. This site has detailed information about saving energy at home, in your business, at school, and in your transportation, as well as links to the "Consumer Guide to Renewable Energy" and "Ask an Energy Expert," where you can inquire about anything that's on your mind. These are some of the ideas you may want to investigate:

- cooling your home naturally
- landscaping for energy efficiency
- do-it-yourself home energy audit
- advanced glazing materials for windows
- launching a community recycling program
- public transportation options

mortgage" programs (EEMs). Here are a few examples of the types of loans available:

- Federal Housing Authority EEMs, insured by another FHA, the Federal Housing Administration, offer up to $8,000 in extra loan money with no income requirements or additional down payment.

- Veterans can apply for EEMs in any amount approved by the Depart-

ment of Veterans Affairs, up to 90 percent of the home's appraised value.

- Newly constructed homes with an Energy Star are 30 percent more energy efficient than standard homes. An Energy Star mortgage allows borrowers to stretch the amount of money they can borrow in relation to their income by 2 percent or more and offers other incentives as well.

- Fannie Mae Energy Efficiency Improvement Loans offer interest rates below market for loans of up to 10 years.

With so many sources of financing, you only have yourself to blame if your energy bills remain sky high. For more information, go to www.eren.doe.gov/erec/factsheets/feehome.html, or call the Energy Efficiency and Renewable Energy Clearinghouse (EREC) at 800-363-3732.

MONEY TO PRESERVE WETLANDS

If you have a wetland or stream on your property, the U.S. Fish and Wildlife Service may pay you to restore it as a wildlife habitat. The Partners for Fish and Wildlife Program has already helped to restore almost a million acres to top-quality habitats for mammals, birds, and fish. Assistance offered by the program ranges from simple advice all the way to design and funding of full restoration projects. Some of the projects funded by the Partners program include:

- restoring wetland water control systems

- planting native trees, shrubs, and grasslands

- creating off-stream livestock watering

- removing exotic plants and animals

- prescribed burning

To find out if your property qualifies, contact the U.S. Fish and Wildlife Service, Division of Fish and Wildlife Management Assistance, 400 Arlington Square, 1849 C Street NW, Washington, D.C. 20240, or call 703-358-2161. Detailed information is also available at partners.fws.gov.

KEEP AMERICA BEAUTIFUL

If you see illegal dumping or any other pollution happening, the Environmental Protection Agency wants to know. Report your tip at es.epa.gov/oeca/main/

enforce/file.html. There may be a reward for information—up to $10,000 under the Comprehensive Environmental Response Compensation and Liability Act. Polluters, watch your backs!

$$ FOR SMALL BUSINESS

The Small Business Administration (SBA) has no other mission but to help small businesses succeed. A dizzying number of loan and equity financing opportunities are explained at the group's Web site: www.sba.gov/financing. Small-business advice and free workshops are offered at the SBA's Small Business Development Centers and Women's Business Development Centers in large and medium-size cities throughout the country. The needs of women, minority, and franchise business owners are the focus of special SBA programs. For the location of your nearest Business Development Center, go to www.sba.gov/sbdc, or call the SBA Answer Desk at 800-UASK-SBA (827-5722).

DID FREE TRADE KILL YOUR JOB?

Generous benefits are available to workers whose jobs have evaporated due to foreign trade competition. Up to four months of retraining and job placement, plus income replacement after unemployment compensation runs out, are just a few of the benefits. But you (or your employer or union) have to file a petition with the Department of Labor to receive them.

Here's where to get the Petition for Trade Adjustment Assistance:

- Visit your local State Employment Security Agency.

- Call 202-693-3560.

- Write to U.S. Department of Labor, Employment and Training Administration, Division of Trade Adjustment Assistance,

200 Constitution Avenue NW, Room C-5311, Washington, D.C. 20210.

- Visit wdsc.doleta.gov/ trade_act/petitions.asp online.

Caution: Do not submit a petition more than 60 days before your scheduled layoff. It will probably be rejected.

WHAT YOU'LL SEE ON THE NEW GED

This exam, which allows people who quit school to qualify as high school grads, has been totally revised as of 2002. The new test isn't harder, but it is different. The good news is that you can prepare for the test by living your daily life. The new reading test includes memos, letters, and flyers like you might get in the mail. The math test can involve tasks such as comparing this year's electric bill to last year's. Consumer skills include understanding labels on food products, determining what is the better buy, and deciding what is the better option if, for example, you are on a sodium-free diet. The test even uses information out of employee manuals from Taco Bell, Safeway, and Red Lobster, similar to the paperwork

TOP SECRET

A few quick facts about money:

- The U.S. one-dollar bill is the most-used bill in the United States.

- The U.S. $20 bill is the most-counterfeited bill in the United States.

- The U.S. $100 bill is the most-used bill outside of the United States, followed closely by the U.S. $50 bill.

- One-dollar bills cost 3.9 cents to produce.

- Five-dollar bills cost 5.3 cents to produce.

- The other bills, $10, $20, $50 and $100, cost 6.8 cents to produce. They cost more because of the very expensive color-shifting ink in the lower right-hand numeral.

they hand you on the first day of work.

REWARD FROM THE TAX MAN

If you know people who are cheating on their taxes, you can receive up to 15 percent of the tax they owe. Ask your tax professional to fill out Form 211, Application for Reward for Original Information. You'll have to get it in hard copy because you won't find it on the IRS's Web site.

REWARDS FOR GOOD CITIZENS

Reporting other kinds of criminal activity can also net you cash, if your information leads to a seizure of illegal goods or an arrest. Here's who you're gonna call:

- For suspected drug activity, contact the Drug Enforcement Administration field office in your area. You can find the phone number in the government section of your phone book. Rewards are given on a case-by-case basis.

- For any type of crime that involves crossing the U.S. border, such as smuggling, counterfeit goods imports, terrorism, child pornography, or Internet crime, you can phone your tip to the U.S. Customs Service at 800-BE-ALERT (800-232-2538). Cash rewards for your information are possible.

INSIDER INFO: IT'S WHAT YOU KNOW THAT COUNTS

★ ★ ★ ★

OUR GOVERNMENT is in the business of gathering information. Most of it, such as income tax returns and campaign finance disclosures, is collected to make sure that individuals and corporations are following the law. But there are also millions of pages of reports created by government agencies that contain useful information for you. Thankfully, because of the Freedom of Information Act and the Internet, these secrets have become much more accessible. Here are some of the things you can find out.

WHERE IN THE UNITED STATES?

Whether you're looking for the town where your dad grew up or just want to know where something in the news is happening, the U.S. Geologic Survey can help. Its database of geographic names holds current and historic location data for almost any U.S. geographic feature you might want. You can search for them at: geonames.usgs. gov/pls/gnis/web_query. gnis_web_query_form. For the location of the town where Dad grew up, look under "populated place" or "post office." The database also contains cemeteries, churches, streams, forests, mountains, and 56 other geographic features to include in your search. Once you've found an area of interest, you can look at several different maps. You may also request a database search by mail or phone. For this service, contact: Geographic Names Information, Branch of Geographic Names, U.S. Geological Survey, 12201 Sunrise Valley Dr., Reston, VA 20192; 888-ASK-USGS.

GIVE A HOOT

Is your home near a source of pollution? The U.S. Environmental Protection Agency (EPA) has made that information—and much more—available through its Web site. You can search for sources of pollution and even heavily polluted Superfund sites by zip code at www.epa.gov/epahome/comm.htm and www.epa.gov/superfund/sites. You can also discover environmental facts about the watershed area where you live at www.epa.gov/surfnewi/text.html. This Web site also lets you join thousands of people working to protect local environments through an "Adopt Your Watershed" program, where you can find "Fifteen Things You Can Do to Make a Difference in Your Watershed."

SAFE TO DRINK?

The EPA wants you to know about the water that flows from your tap. You can examine your state's drinking water compliance report and find out about any problems with your local water system at www.epa.gov/safewater/swinfo.htm. Or you can discover the same information by calling the Safe Drinking Water Hotline at 800-426-4791.

In addition, you can request, or download, a copy of "Water on Tap: A Consumer's Guide to the Nation's Drinking Water." This brochure answers several important questions:

- Where does drinking water come from?

- How can you tell if your drinking water is safe?

- How can you protect your drinking water?

- What should you do if there's a problem with your water?

Consumers whose water comes from wells can also find helpful guidelines at www.epa.gov/safewater/pwells1.html or from the Safe Drinking Water Hotline.

YOU CAN GARDEN WITHOUT CHEMICALS

The EPA encourages landscaping with native wildflowers and grasses. Once established, they require no fertilizers, herbicides, pesticides, or watering. And a natural garden will attract birds, butterflies, and other animals. Tips on how to get started can be found at www.epa.gov/greenacres. You'll also find information on how to fight local "weed laws" if neighbors insist on green-lawn conformity.

EWWW...TAINTED FOOD

With all the food-borne illnesses in the news today, it's hard to know what's safe to eat. The U.S. Department of Agriculture and the Food and Drug Administration feel your pain—and want to prevent your next bellyache. Live operators are standing by during normal business hours, and recorded information is available 24 hours a day. So if you've got questions, here are the numbers to call:

TOP SECRET

Head Start is designed to help low-income kids get ahead, but 10 percent of kids in the program can be from families with incomes above poverty guidelines. Officials particularly want to include children with special needs, including language problems and motor-skill disabilities. For more information go to www2.acf.dhhs.gov/programs/hsb, click on "Frequently Asked Questions," and enter "eligibility" into the search engine.

- USDA's Meat and Poultry Hotline, 800-535-4555 (press 6 for product recalls and news)

- National Center for Nutrition and Dietetics Consumer Nutrition Hotline, 800-366-1655

- Center for Food Safety and Applied Nutrition, Food and Drug Administration, 800-332-4010

TOTAL RECALL

You have a right to expect that the products you buy won't hurt you. The U.S. Consumer Product Safety Commission (CPSC) protects that right by pressuring companies into recalling items that have been proven unsafe. You can find out about current or past recalls at www.cpsc.gov/cpscpub/prerel/prerel.html or by calling 800-638-2772. Recently recalled products have included:

- flammable children's sleepware

- children's cargo pants with breakable buttons, a choking hazard

- strollers that often collapse

Many recalls are a direct response to consumer complaints. If you have experienced or know of any product injuries, report them at www.cpsc.gov/talk.html, or call the CPSC number during business hours. The CPSC does not handle complaints about cars, tires, car seats, foods, medicines, or cosmetics, but its Web site links to other sites that do.

BLOWING THE WHISTLE: IS IT SAFE?

Waste and fraud in government are almost routine news stories. But we might not know nearly as much about them without the

Whistle-Blower Protection Law, passed unanimously by Congress in 1989. The law was intended to protect employees from retaliation for reporting illegal actions they observe. In recent years, however, its protections have been gutted by court rulings. A recent survey found that 41 percent of employees did not report misconduct they had witnessed because they feared the consequences. But legislation is currently before Congress to significantly strengthen the law. For more information, see www.whistleblower.org or call the Government Accountability Project at 202-408-0034.

WHAT THE GOVERNMENT HAS TO TELL YOU

The Freedom of Information Act (FOIA) is the public's open sesame to the inner workings of the government. Records must be made available to the public unless there is some compelling reason to keep them secret. "We're the government, and we don't want to tell you" has not been a good enough reason since FOIA became law more than 30 years ago. There are only nine reasons

DO YOU HAVE AN FBI FILE?

Speaking of files, is it possible the FBI has one on *you*? It is, if you were ever fingerprinted, involved in a protest of any kind, or simply came into contact with the wrong people. A request under the Freedom of Information Act (FOIA) is all you need to blast your file loose, although you may have to wait a while to receive it because the FBI is swamped with requests from people who want to know how closely Big Brother has been watching. Recently, though, the agency has posted its most-requested files in its "Electronic Reading Room" at foia.fbi.gov/room.htm. Here's where you can find what the FBI had to say about Marilyn Monroe, Elvis, James Dean, Al Capone, and more. It's fascinating reading.

Want to Stay out of Jail? Learn to Read

Prisoners as a group are not like most people walking down the street. There are many differences, of course, but according to the U.S. Department of Justice, one is that most prisoners can't read:

- More than 50 percent of all adults in state and federal correctional facilities cannot read or write.

- Only about one-third of those in prison have completed high school.

- The typical male inmate functions two or three grade levels below the grade level actually completed in school.

On top of that, the U.S. Department of Education reports:

- Depending upon the definition of literacy, as many as 75 percent of prisoners cannot read.

- Among juvenile offenders, 85 percent have reading problems.

the government can use for withholding information. Among them are:

- national security (under presidential order)

- trade secrets

- hindrance of law enforcement

TOP SECRET

Every government agency must now post its "most requested" FOIA documents on its Web site. It's the law.

- "clearly unwarranted invasion of personal privacy"

That last reason means you can't get the government to tell you about the deadbeat your sister's been dating or about your neighbor's shady past.

You can learn a lot about what the government knows about your vicinity, your employer, your environment, and much more. The more specific you are about the records you want, the more likely you are to get them. The best approach is simply to ask the agency most likely to have the information to give it to you. In a surprising number of cases, the information you might want has already been published and is freely available. But if you need to file a Freedom of Information request, the Reporters Committee for Freedom of the Press has made it easy for anyone to do. Simply fill out the Automated FOI Letter Generator at www.rcfp.org/foi_lett.html.

For more details about FOIA, request the booklet "Your Right to Federal Records" through the National Contact Center at 800-688-9889, or download it from the Federal Programs page at www.pueblo.gsa.gov.

UNCLE SAM WANTS YOU: TO VOLUNTEER

Are you ready for adventure? Whatever you want to do, your government is eager to find a way to help you do it. Hundreds of volunteer opportunities can be found at www.hud.gov when you hit the "Volunteering" link. You can also call 202-708-1112 to be directed to a host of volunteer positions. Some of the ways you can contribute are:

• Join Senior Corps, for people over 55, and help children learn to read.

• Volunteer for Earth Science Corps, and help map your community.

• Sign up for Neighborhood Networks, and bring computer skills to urban areas.

• Go to "Indian Country," and volunteer your talents to Native Americans.

If you'd rather volunteer overseas, the Volunteering page also has links to the Peace Corps and the International Executive Service Corps, which sends managers to other coun-

PEACE CORPS DROPOUTS ADD UP

The Peace Corps may be "the toughest job you'll ever love," but make sure you know what you're getting into before you sign up. For a lot of people it's too tough and they don't love it. The Peace Corps averages a 27-29 percent "early return rate." That's bureaucratic for failure rate. Some people decide on their own, and others have the Peace Corps itself decide for them, that they aren't cut out for the hardships that are part of life in developing countries.

Peace Corps volunteers may make the world a better place, but their two years in a foreign country aren't the kind of trips that travel posters are made of. They may very well have an assignment with no electricity, phones, running water, or indoor plumbing.

tries for short-term, English-language assignments.

IT'S A BIG, BAD WORLD

You can find out what spies know about every country around the world from *The World Factbook,* compiled by the CIA. Here you'll find the real deal on the geography, people, government, economy, and defense of countries and regions around the world. The latest edition is available on the net at www.cia.gov. You may download it for free or order a bound copy for $83 from: Superintendent of Documents, P.O. Box 371954, Pittsburgh, PA 15250-7954; 202-512-1800.

If you're going to travel the world, be sure to go online to visit travel.state.gov/travel_warnings.html before you go. Here you'll find much more than travel warnings. For each country in the world, a "consular information sheet" is packed with important facts for the traveler, including entry requirements, safety information, common types of crime, medical facilities, road and airport conditions, and consulate addresses. You may also contact the State Department's Bureau of Consular Affairs, Office of American Citizen Services, 202-647-5225 for additional travel information. Don't leave home without it.

Outrageous Government Giveaways to Big Business

The richest property owner in America is the government. And when it wants to give something away—or sell it for less-than-market value—it does. It's not surprising that those who give the most to political campaigns—corporations and their executives—also benefit most from government generosity. Here are some of the most amazing giveaways we found:

- The FCC gave licenses for digital television to broadcasters for free. Those licenses are estimated to be worth as much as $70 billion.

- The 1872 Mining Act—still on the books!—lets mining companies buy federal land for $5 per acre or less. And they don't have to pay royalties on the minerals they extract.

- The Market Promotion Program of the Department of Agriculture spends $90 million per year to help companies like Sunkist and Ocean Spray promote their products abroad. Why do these profitable companies need help?

- The Forest Service gives $45 million to private timber companies to build roads in national forests.

To see what else your tax dollars are supporting, take a look at grants to businesses at www.cfda.gov/federalcommons/business.html.

Buy the Book

Want help with a problem? Want to know what the government's up to? The U.S. Government Printing

Office (GPO) has 12,000 books to help you. On their Web site, www.access.gpo.gov/su_docs/index.html, a search on the word "home" brings to light helpful publications on home health care, home repair, home mortgages, and more. You can even buy a copy of the federal budget that everyone in Washington always seems to be arguing about. The GPO prints a ton of art books, too—many based on its collections of photographs—and all are coffee-table ready.

In addition to its online ordering, the GPO has 22 regional bookstores located in major cities. Look in the "U.S. Government" section of your phone book, or visit bookstore.gpo.gov/locations/index.html for a list of bookstore addresses.

AND ANYTHING ELSE WORTH KNOWING

Any time you have a question about a government agency, program, or benefit, you can call 800-688-9889 weekdays and talk to a knowledgeable person who will point you in the right direction. Call anytime between 9 A.M. and 8 P.M. Eastern Time, except holidays, and you'll either get an answer right away or be directed to someone who can help you. At other times, you'll be able to choose from recordings of frequently asked questions.

HEALTH SECRETS

★ ★ ★ ★

ONE OF THE responsibilities of our government is to maintain the public health by safeguarding its citizens from harmful drugs and unhealthy products. The government is more successful in accomplishing this in some cases than in others. No one really expects them to be 100-percent effective, but some of these policies make more sense than others.

TOBACCO IS NOT REGULATED BY THE FDA

The Food and Drug Administration (FDA) has authority to regulate all the food and drugs in the country. But they do not regulate tobacco products. Why? It's not food—OK. It's not alcohol—also OK. But tobacco, and most particularly the nicotine in tobacco, is not a drug? Not according to the FDA, no. And if there's no drug involved with tobacco or its production, then tobacco companies do not need to disclose any information—to either the government or the public—about the ingredients or additives they use. How did this happen? Who decided that tobacco wasn't a drug? The answer, as is often the situation with government,

TOP SECRET

More than half the money needed to bring top-selling prescription drugs to market came from U.S. taxpayers and *not* from investment by the drug industry. So why is the cost of medicine so high?

TOBACCO INDUSTRY SLEEPING WITH THE ENEMY—THE CDC

Recently, the tobacco industry has decided to foot the bill for some government programs aimed at preventing tobacco use by youth. Not surprisingly, this has caused some controversy. Should government accept tobacco money even if it's for a good cause? The Centers for Disease Control and Prevention (CDC) has decided to work with the tobacco industry and has made public its internal guidelines for collaborating with the private sector. Keep your eye out for those TV ads and let the CDC know your opinion about what you see. You can contact the agency through its Web site, www.cdc.gov/tobacco.

comes down to *politics* and *money*.

The *U.S. Pharmacopoeia,* an official listing of drugs in the United States, included tobacco until 1905, when pressure from tobacco-state legislators forced the publication to eliminate the listing in all future editions. This date is particularly significant because the 1906 Food and Drug Act covered all drugs listed in the 1906 edition of the *Pharmacopoeia.* Guess what substance dodged regulation?

Tobacco has been a major source of revenue to both state and federal govern-

ments. Throughout history, the tobacco industry has barely been restricted by government regulation of

TOP SECRET

As if nicotine itself wasn't bad enough—cigarettes can contain at least 599 other additives. No one regulates what they put in or how much they put in. Rumors surface from time to time about urine being one of those secret ingredients. Well, as part of a major settlement agreement, the tobacco industry must now disclose what these ingredients are, and you can find them listed on the Web site www.drugs.indiana.edu/druginfo/additives.html.

any kind. Three million people, roughly 750,000 families, receive $1.4 billion annually through jobs related to tobacco cultivation and production. That's a lot of taxpayers.

But the situation seems to be changing now. Why? Once again, the answer is *politics* and *money*. It is now clear to the public that smoking kills, so people are clamoring for government action. Add to that the fact that tax revenues from tobacco have about maxed out. The excise tax is not based on a percentage of the sale price, but on a rate for each pack. Despite the fact that tobacco prices have gone up, tax revenue has not increased accordingly. In fact, taxes have declined by more than 70 percent. The combination of public demand for action and lower revenue has made the tobacco companies an easy target for government regulators.

EXPERIMENTAL DRUGS—FREE!

If you suffer from any disease that is not responding to treatment, you may want to join a clinical trial. Researchers all over the country are testing new drugs for fighting diseases ranging from seasonal affective disorder to cancer. Although such trials come with caveats that will be discussed below, many people have received useful and beneficial medical treatment through them.

You will not be guaranteed a cure…many of these drugs are just out of the test tube. And about half of the subjects in any study will receive a placebo—that is, a harmless, powerless fake drug—because scientists need something to compare the tested drug against. But drug trials offer a ray of hope to patients who cannot find effective treatment and, perhaps just as important, a chance to contribute to the possibility of finding a cure for your disease.

The Internet has made it easy to find a government-sponsored clinical trial.

- Go to clinicaltrials.gov for National Institutes of Health studies; hit "Focused Search" to search by age.

- Surf over to www.actis. org for AIDS/HIV trials.

- Try cancertrials.nci.nih. gov for all types of cancer studies.

You can also call the Cancer Information Service at 800-4-CANCER to get additional information about cancer trials. To find out more about all types of clinical trials, call the Food and Drug Administration's Office of Special Health Issues at 301-827-4460.

MISCONDUCT IN MEDICAL RESEARCH

And now for the bad news. The government funds or sponsors thousands of clinical trials and other types of medical research each year. Sometimes things go wrong. When misconduct is suspected in taxpayer-funded medical research, the usual complaint, inquiry, investigation, and appeal process can take months or years.

Sometimes, however, that process gets totally cast aside. When a healthy 24-year-old woman died during a 2001 asthma study at Johns Hopkins University, government regulators jumped in immediately to cut off funding for all medical research at the university to the tune of $300 million. Hopkins promised to tighten up on some procedures to protect subjects and—after only four days—the funding was restored on a conditional basis. That's not even a billing

TOP SECRET

No more Ouchies! The FDA is considering a flu nasal spray to replace the old standby flu shots.

cycle. At the time, Hopkins was conducting about 2,800 government-funded research studies using tens of thousands of human subjects.

UNSATISFACTORY SAFEGUARDS IN VETERANS HOSPITAL

One hospital in Los Angeles, the West Los Angeles VA Healthcare Center, was found to have performed human research without obtaining proper legal consent from the patients. Specifically, heart research was conducted on patients who not only did not give consent but who refused consent. One patient was subjected to a prolonged high-risk procedure during more routine surgery after having refused consent twice. Another died in the hospital parking lot after taking an experimental drug. The National Institutes of Health (NIH) canceled the hospital's research contract and called for independent audits. Complaints and reports of noncompliance

have surfaced against hospitals in Cincinnati, Tampa, and Philadelphia as well.

Medical research is a routine activity at nearly all 173 veterans hospitals across the nation. The NIH watchdog agency claims its office has dozens of investigations open at any given time.

GOVERNMENT PROCEDURES TO ADDRESS MEDICAL MISCONDUCT

What's the normal procedure for establishing the safety of research subjects? According to publications from the Department of Health and Human Service's Office of Research and

TOP SECRET

Each year an estimated 4.7 million Americans suffer the trauma of dog bites. Nearly two million of those victims are small children. According to the Centers for Disease Control in Atlanta, dog bites have become the number-one public health risk for children. Children are 900 times more likely to be bitten by dogs than are mail carriers.

Permanent Home for Mutant Mice Established

No, it's not a new cartoon character. There are more than 3,000 strains of mutant mice that have been created during research by the National Institutes of Health (NIH). Scientists sometimes need such mice for their research, so the Mutant Mouse Regional Resource Center (MMRRC) National Network will now function as a one-stop shop for them.

But how did these mice get to be mutant? Through genetic research. Scientists create the mice mutations by turning particular genes on or off or by inserting foreign genes into the mouse genome. Not all such mice are always used in research, however, and laboratories from all over the country are donating their leftover mice to form a sort of mouse bank from which other researchers can draw. In order to preserve them, the mouse embryos are essentially frozen until they are needed.

If you're curious for more information, go online to the mouse bank Web site at www.mmrrc.org.

Integrity (ORI), there is basically a promise, what the ORI calls an "assurance," by the research institution to safeguard human safety. This assurance isn't like a vow or swearing in or even signing a document; it is simply inherent in the process of applying for a research grant. According to the ORI itself, "An institution establishes an assurance when an official signs the face-page of the [Public Health Service] grant application form or when the institution files a separate assurance form." Another agency, the Office for Human Research Protections (OHRP), was established in 2000 specifically to oversee human research, but it is also not a preventive agency. Both the ORI and OHRP have pages and pages of guidelines for handling complaints. If you're interested, you can read these documents at their Web sites, ori.dhhs.gov and ohrp.osophs.dhhs.gov.

That's basically all there is to the government's oversight of medical research. There seems to be an assumption on the part of many citizens that the government takes a more hands-on approach—especially with research involving human subjects. But there is no direct oversight of projects and very few inspections. The system relies on watchdog reports, internal audits, and public information that appears in the news. There is no prevention—any government monitoring is done after the fact. Theoretically, people could die, and if no one complained nor did it become public, that government-funded research would continue.

FLUORIDE—THE GOVERNMENT-APPROVED POISON

Fluoride has been banned in many countries, yet in the United States they still keep pumping it into the water supply. Fluoride is not a nutrient, it is not essential, and it may even damage your health.

FLUORIDE AVOIDANCE ADVICE

- Don't drink out of aluminum cans.
- Don't cook with aluminum pots.
- Check out where your bottled water comes from, and don't pay to poison yourself.
- Find out if your local water is fluoridated, and fight to get it stopped.

Although scientists continue to disagree, some studies have linked fluoride to cancer, increased osteoporosis, Alzheimer's disease, and other serious ailments. And instead of preventing cavities, it may actually cause them! A study at the University of Arizona showed that the more fluoridated water children drank, the more cavities they had. Even the Environmental Protection Agency (EPA) has gotten into the act, listing fluoride as a contaminant in drinking water.

The EPA doesn't allow more than 4 milligrams of fluoride per liter of water. The FDA has also weighed in, requiring the following warning label to appear on all tubes of toothpaste: **"Keep out of reach of children under 6 years of age.** If you accidentally swallow more than used for brushing, seek professional help or contact a poison control center immediately."

Taxpayer dollars are being used to fluoridate the water supply unnecessarily—even despite these potentially serious health hazards. If the fluoridation equipment were to break down, it could possibly poison a whole town.

So why is it in our nation's water supply? Fluoride is a waste by-product of the aluminum manufacturing process, and in the 1940s, there was no legal way to dispose of large quantities of it. Did someone come up with the idea of selling fluoride to the public, telling them it would be good for their teeth?

SOCIAL SECURITY AND DISABILITY SECRETS

★ ★ ★ ★

MOST PEOPLE have paid into Social Security all their working lives. And most of them are completely in the dark about how much they should expect to receive when they retire. Worse, some people think they won't get anything at all, especially if they are young and just entering the work force. For the insider scoop, read on. You'll also see how Social Security and other programs can help if you become disabled.

HOW MUCH WILL YOU GET?

Social Security was never designed to make anyone rich. If you retired today, you would receive Social Security payments of between $3,000 and $17,000 per year. The amount you will actually qualify for depends on:

• your date of birth

• your lifetime earnings

• how old you are when you retire

Your Social Security benefit also depends on how many "quarters" (three-month periods) you worked at jobs covered by Social Security.

Upon request, the Social Security Administration (SSA) will send you a Statement of Earnings that de-

When Can You Retire and Receive Social Security?

New rules say that only people born in 1937 and before will be able to retire at age 65 and receive full benefits. If you turn 65 in the year 2002 or have already turned 65, that means you. After that, retirement age gets progressively later until those born in 1960 must wait until age 67 before receiving full benefits. Here's a chart to explain it all.

Your Year of Birth	Your Full Retirement Age
1937 or before	65
1938	65 and 2 months
1939	65 and 4 months
1940	65 and 6 months
1941	65 and 8 months
1942	65 and 10 months
1943–1954	66
1955	66 and 2 months
1956	66 and 4 months
1957	66 and 6 months
1958	66 and 8 months
1959	66 and 10 months
1960 and later	67

If you retire before your full retirement age or if you become disabled, you will receive a lower monthly benefit for life.

tails your estimated retirement and disability benefit. But you can also figure your benefit yourself on the Internet at www.ssa.gov/planners/calculators.htm.

TOP SECRET

With Social Security, 11 percent of retirees live in poverty. Without it, 40 percent would.

One of the forms there also allows you to include an estimate of your future earnings in the calculation.

Set the Record Straight

If you receive a Statement of Earnings, check it to make sure it accurately reflects what you've earned over the years. If it's wrong, you should take immediate steps to correct it. The SSA only allows you to challenge your earnings data if you have the records to prove your case. If the discrepancy concerns income from too long ago, your records may be lost. That's why it's important to check the Statement of Earnings and, if necessary, correct it as soon as possible. The people most likely to find errors on their Social Security statements are the self-employed and joint filers, who may find income is misapplied between spouses.

To dispute your Statement of Earnings, you should call the SSA at 800-772-1213 and request a review. You have 60 days to appeal this review if you still disagree with the determination. You may do this by mail or in person at your local Social Security Office. You can find out more about the Statement of Earnings online at www.ssa.gov/mystatement.

ONE BENEFIT OR TWO?

Women, if you're married and worked outside the home, here's a question you may pose at retirement: Will your benefits be based on your own work account or your husband's?

When Social Security began, most women didn't work outside the home. Therefore, Social Security provides a "spouse's benefit" of 50 percent of the

APPLYING FOR SOCIAL SECURITY ONLINE

No more lines at the Social Security Administration office! Well, sure, there are still lines there, but you don't have to stand in them. Just answer a series of questions that you can find at www.ssa.gov (click on "Apply for Social Security benefits online"), and you'll start receiving your money. You can even begin your application, then return to it later if you don't have all the information you need. Once you've filled them out, you'll need a printer so you can print out the forms, sign them, and mail them in.

husband's benefit to all women who wish to take it. (Husbands also qualify for the spouse's benefit if their wives earned significantly more than they did.) In other words, married couples receiving the spouse's benefit get a full benefit plus 50 percent.

On the other hand, if you are a wife who did work outside the home, your benefits are based on your own work record, and both you and your spouse can receive a full benefit at age 65. Whether yours is more than you would have received from the "spouse's benefit" depends on how much you have worked and the salary you received. If you've earned about the same as your spouse over your working lives, you'll both receive about the same size benefit. If you would make more with the spouse's benefit, the SSA will pay you your own benefit and then dip into the spouse's benefit to make up the difference. The SSA tries to pay you the full amount that you're entitled to.

To find out more about Social Security benefits for husbands and wives, request a free booklet, "Social Security: What Every Woman Should Know," by calling the Federal Consumer Information Center at 800-688-9889.

SOCIAL SECURITY PRIVATIZATION— A GOOD DEAL?

In recent years, Social Security has run a large surplus. Any surplus Social

Security may have is invested in Treasury bonds that help pay down the national debt. But would it be a bad idea to invest a portion of Social Security funds in something that earns a little more, like the stock market? Here are some reasons to question that idea:

- Guaranteed benefits would be reduced.

- Every transaction would be subject to brokerage commissions.

- Trillions of extra dollars competing in the market would mean even more violent gyrations in security prices.

- What goes up can also go down.

Incentives for private retirement savings can be created without tapping into Social Security revenues. Of course, that wouldn't be as exciting a prospect for the investment companies salivating to get their hands on some Social

WHAT IS THE SOCIAL SECURITY "TRUST FUND"?

Actually, there's no such thing as a Social Security Trust Fund, despite what you may have heard from Washington. The money that is paid into Social Security by today's workers is paid out to today's retirees almost immediately. However, today's workers pay more in Social Security taxes than is needed by retirees, and that's what causes the surplus.

But that surplus is not sitting in a bank or a "lockbox" anywhere. *By law,* it is given to the Treasury to spend as it sees fit, such as on Social Security benefits, or tanks, or…whatever, including paying down the national debt. The only thing in any sort of "trust fund" are government IOUs (Treasury bonds). But the government promises to pay you a benefit when you retire—they'll get the money from the taxes of people who are working at that time and from other government revenues. And the government will, you can count on that. Can you imagine the gray-haired riot in Washington if Social Security was actually allowed to die?

Security money—or for the politicians salivating to get their hands on donations from those companies. Count on continuing debate.

SOCIAL SECURITY SCAMS

Politicians aside, a lot of people like to play with the truth where Social Security is concerned. Many times, Social Security scams come in official-looking envelopes. They offer to provide some service—like helping you apply for benefits—in exchange for a fee. The scam comes when you learn that these services are free from the federal government. Another trick is to say you can be eligible for extra money from the government if you send in a deposit or a form giving them your Social Security number. If you get any offers like these, keep this in mind: The government never charges for services related to Social Security. And the government already knows your Social Security number.

WHAT IF YOU'RE DISABLED?

It's not just truck drivers and pilots who are at risk of being disabled. Incredibly, the average worker has a 30-percent chance of being disabled between the first day of work and the day of retirement. But few people know that they can receive Social Security disability benefits even if they are not permanently disabled.

What Social Security will not pay for is if you are only partially disabled or are disabled for less than a year. Also, you must be unable to do *any* kind of work. If you can't be an accountant anymore but can still dig ditches, for instance, the SSA won't consider you disabled and won't pay.

Social Security disability benefits can begin six months after you become disabled, but you should apply as soon after you become disabled as possible. You will automatically be enrolled in Medicare two years after your disability payments begin. The amount you will receive, like Social Security benefits, depends on your lifetime earnings before you were disabled. An estimate of your disability benefit will appear on your Social Security Statement of Earnings.

For more information about Social Security disability benefits, visit your local SSA office, go to www.ssa.gov/pubs/10029.html, or call the SSA at 800-772-1213.

TICKET TO WORK

Under a new law called "Ticket to Work," disabled people no longer have to choose between health care and work. In 2000, Medicare and Medicaid were expanded to cover more working people with disabilities, so those workers no longer must depend on a private employer to provide sometimes-expensive health care and insurance. In addition, people collecting Social Security disability benefits or Supplemental Security Income (SSI) will receive a "ticket" that will give them voluntary access to:

• employment services

• vocational rehabilitation services

• disability support services

The program began rolling out in 13 states in 2001 and will be phased in nationwide throughout the next three years. Disabled people will automatically receive their "ticket" and benefits booklet when they become eligible for the program.

EARLY RETIREMENT MONEY—WITHOUT PENALTY

Taking money from your retirement accounts before age 59½ usually results in an extra "early distribution tax" of 10 percent. But if you're *permanently* disabled, you can take that money without penalty, al-

MAJESTIC AMERICA—FOR FREE

If you are eligible to receive federal disability benefits, you also qualify for a Golden Access Passport: a free lifetime pass to national parks, monuments, historic sites, recreation areas, and national wildlife refuges. You'll also get a 50-percent discount on fees that may be charged for activities like parking and boat launching. To receive a Golden Access Passport, all you need to do is show proof of permanent disability. Your Social Security disability notice is best, but you can also use a veteran's card, a Medicaid card, a letter from a federal agency, or any other proof of medically determined permanent disability.

Golden Access Passports are available at the gates of any national area where an entrance fee is charged—but don't forget your proof of disability. Your family is also admitted free when they are with you. To find out if a park is accessible to the disabled, visit ParkNet (www.nps.gov) and search the site by park name.

though you'll still have to pay regular income tax on what you withdraw. Because the IRS follows the same definitions of *disabled* as the SSA, the easiest way to prove you qualify is to attach your Social Security disability notice to your return in any year you make a withdrawal. Otherwise, the IRS might determine your disability is not permanent or long-lasting and charge you the penalty anyway. Whenever you withdraw your money, discuss your situation with your plan administrator so your action can be correctly reported to the IRS.

MONEY FOR HOSPITAL CARE

Hospitals that accept federal funds for expansion or remodeling under the Hill-Burton program must offer free or reduced-cost care to qualified low-income patients. A family of four earning less than $17,650 per year in 2001 and not covered by Medicaid or private health insurance is eligible for Hill-Burton. Physicians' fees, drugs, and certain hospital services are not covered, however. For more information, 24 hours a day, call the Hill-Burton Hotline at 800-638-0742 (800-492-0359 for residents of Maryland).

MEDICARE AND HOSPICE CARE

In the end, we're all going to want loving care. If you or a loved one are covered by Medicare Part A, that care can be provided by a hospice. No heroic measures are covered, just medicine to maximize comfort. And many times the care of doctors, nurses, home health aids, and other workers can be provided in the home, at absolutely no cost. There are only a few restrictions on the patient:

• The patient must be diagnosed with less than six months to live.

• The patient must sign a statement to choose hospice care over routine Medicare benefits for the particular terminal disease.

• The hospice must be Medicare approved.

For more information, call 800-MEDICARE or visit www.medicare.gov.

You Deserve It: Great Deals for Seniors and Vets Only

★ ★ ★ ★

As you enter your golden years, Uncle Sam isn't about to forget you. That goes double if you've served in the military. Veterans and people over 55 qualify for some well-deserved discounts and government benefits available to no one else—benefits that go far beyond Medicare and Social Security. Too bad that most people (until now) have never heard of them. Maybe that's why the government can afford to provide these services free or for little cost. Shhh. Don't tell anyone.

Need a Legal Eagle?

Uncle Sam wants you to be able to talk to a lawyer when you need one. The government provides funding to local Area Agencies on Aging to provide free legal services to those over 60 who are unable to afford a private attorney for noncriminal cases. To find out if you qualify, call your Area Agency on Aging, listed in the government section of your phone book. For more general information, you can browse the National Association of Area Agencies on Aging's Web site at www.n4a.org.

Twenty-one states (along with the District of Columbia and Puerto Rico) now offer hotlines to help people over 60 (over 50 in Pennsylvania) with legal questions, and more states are expected to launch similar hotlines soon. The lawyers on these hotlines do not offer representation themselves, but they will provide advice and referrals to legal service programs or private attorneys. For the current list of state hotline numbers, go to the Web site of the Department of Health and Human Service's Administration on Aging, www.aoa.gov/legal/hotline.html.

ELDER LAW

In addition to the state hotlines, many specialists in a relatively new legal field called Elder Law provide free initial consultations for those over 65 who have legal difficulties related to their age, such as paying for nursing home care or making Medicare claims. To find an Elder Law attorney in your area, type in your zip code at www. naela. com/applications/ consumerdirectory/index. cfm. And for a free brochure, "Questions and Answers When Looking for an Elder Law Attorney," send a stamped, self-addressed, business-size envelope to National Academy of Elder Law Attorneys, Q & A, 1604 N. Country Club Road, Tucson, AZ 85716-3102. You can also see the brochure online at www. naela.com/naela/questions.htm.

SEE THE U.S.A.—FOR LESS

Want to see the Alaska National Wildlife Refuge? The Everglades? The Grand Canyon? If you're at least 62, you can now see all the magnificent national lands owned by the federal gov-

---

TOP SECRET

Tourists come from all over the world to visit Grand Canyon National Park. But after they get there, they typically average only half an hour actually looking at the canyon. After that, they spend two hours in the gift shops.

ernment without having to pay budget-busting entrance fees. The "Golden Age Passport" is a lifetime pass for free admission to national parks, monuments, historic sites, recreation areas, and national wildlife refuges.

Spouses and children are admitted free if accompanied by a golden-ager. A 50-percent discount is also given to passport holders for many recreational fees such as camping, parking, swimming, and other activities. And a Golden Age Passport costs only $10.

The drawback? It's a small one, but Golden Age Passports are only available *in person* at any federal area where an entrance fee is charged. Proof of age is required. And Golden Age Passports do *not* cover or reduce any fees necessary for a special recreation permit or any fees charged by concessioners.

VETS FLY FREE— WITH LESS WORRY

A new law makes no-cost "space available" flying for veterans much less of a crap shoot. If you're a vet, you know that the military

THE DEFENSE DEPARTMENT'S SECRET WEAPON

If you've been by a supermarket checkout counter lately, you can probably remember what stories were on the cover of the *National Enquirer*. You might have even picked one up and looked at it, as long as you thought no one was looking at you.

That hasn't gone unnoticed by the Department of Defense's Defense Information School. Their students are the people who work with the press and produce military-base publications. They've also had a long history of putting out important information that no one read because the publications looked too boring. No more. Now they use the infamous tabloid as their guide for making stories jump out at you. And the result is the bureaucrats are creating publications that don't look at all bureaucratic. Many of them are not only winning awards—regular people are really reading them, as well.

calls this "Space A." Vets and their families can now reserve a space on military passenger flights up to 24 hours before boarding. You are not guaranteed a seat—passengers on official military business or emergency leave still get first dibs on them. But it's better than the old "wait until departure time to see if there are any seats" method. The program will eventually be in place at military bases worldwide.

TESTING HELP FOR VETERANS

Whether you want a new career as an accountant, electronics technician, personal trainer, or other professional, if you need to take a test for a license or certificate, the G.I. Bill may be able to help. A new law gives veterans taking approved tests (as well as spouses and children of veterans who suffered service-related disability or death) up to $2,000 per exam—but no more than the cost of the test. You don't even have to pass the test to receive the benefit, and you can receive additional benefits if you need to take the test again. There's no limit to the number of approved tests you can take. You may also receive reimbursement for license renewal tests. All you need to do is send a copy of your test results to your regional office of the

WHAT DID YOU DO IN THE WAR, GRANDPA?

During World War II, Uncle Sam sent the boys to the Pacific and to the European theater. He also sent some photographers right along with them. The result was a photo archive with millions of shots of what World War II looked like, both in frontline combat and at the rear. These photos are for sale, starting at $7.00 for an 8×10 glossy. For help finding the image you want, write to: Still Picture Reference (NWCS-Stills Reference,) Room 5360, National Archives at College Park, 8601 Adelphi Road, College Park, MD 20740-6001.

Department of Veterans Affairs (VA). For more information, go online to www.gibill.va.gov/Education/LCweb.htm.

SAVE MONEY ON PRESCRIPTION DRUGS

The federal government isn't in the business of providing low-cost prescription drugs for seniors. (But there is a program for vets, explained below.) That's why the fight in Congress for a Medicare prescription-drug benefit is so important. In the meantime, you can find information on drug programs your state offers at www.medicare.gov/prescription/home.asp. Just type in your zip code and state, then hit "view results" at the bottom of the page.

Another stopgap measure for more affordable prescription drugs is a program sponsored by the Pharmaceutical Research and Manufacturers of America. This organization publishes a directory of drug manufacturers that will provide drugs to doctors for patients who couldn't otherwise afford them. You may look up a drug manufacturer's program at www.phrma.org/searchcures/dpdpap or call for a directory at 800-762-4636.

FINDING YOUR ROOTS— WITH GOVERNMENT HELP

The National Archives offers extensive help locating records of your ancestors. And while this benefit isn't limited to seniors, that's who's doing most of the

DRUGS FOR VETS

If you served your country, you can get prescription drugs for free or for a two-dollar monthly copayment, even if your medical condition is not related to your service. Many veterans have already been automatically enrolled in this program. If you have not, visit any VA health-care facility or benefits center and ask for VA Form 10-10EZ. You may also call the VA's Health Benefits Service Center at 877-222-VETS for a form or find one online at www.va.gov/forms/medical/FormImageFiles/10-10ez.pdf.

NATIONAL ARCHIVES NEAR YOU

The best news is that you don't have to go to Washington to get your hands on family history records. Chances are, you live reasonably close to one of these 29 cities that are home to regional Archives centers or presidential libraries:

- Anchorage, Alaska
- Little Rock, Arkansas
- Laguna Niguel, San Francisco, and Simi Valley, California
- Denver, Colorado
- Atlanta, Georgia
- Chicago, Illinois
- West Branch, Iowa
- Abilene, Kansas
- College Park and Suitland, Maryland
- Boston, Pittsfield, and Waltham, Massachusetts
- Ann Arbor and Grand Rapids, Michigan
- Independence, Kansas City, Lee's Summit, and St. Louis, Missouri
- Hyde Park and New York City, New York
- Dayton, Ohio
- Philadelphia, Pennsylvania
- Austin, College Station, and Ft. Worth, Texas
- Seattle, Washington

For the address and hours of the center nearest you, go to www.nara.gov/nara/gotonara.html or call 301-713-6800. Happy ancestor hunting!

family history research in this country. And vets may be more interested than most in finding family members who served in the military.

At the National Archives, you can find census records, immigration records, passenger lists from docking ships, old photographs, and much more. Usually, you may copy whatever records you find for 50 cents a page or less. Copies of the full military service files of your ancestors may also be available for a fee of

$17 each, a bargain for the wealth of information they usually contain. For a list of family history records you can search, go online to www.nara.gov/genealogy. For full information, request a free booklet called "Using Records in the National Archives for Genealogical Research" by calling 866-325-7208 or by writing the Product Development and Distribution Staff (NWCP), National Archives and Records Administration, Room G-7, 700 Pennsylvania Avenue NW, Washington, D.C. 20408.

THE LAST, BEST HONOR

No-cost burial in a national cemetery is offered by the VA to honorably discharged veterans, their unremarried spouses, and minor or mentally disabled children. These benefits include a grave site, the burial flag, a headstone, and a Presidential Memorial Certificate. Grave sites may not be reserved in advance, however. Families may request National Cemetery burial through their funeral home, which can also request burial with full military honors, if desired. Just make sure your relatives know where your military records are, as they'll be needed for you to qualify for the honor you deserve.

YOUR RIGHTS AS AN EMPLOYEE

★ ★ ★ ★

IT'S WELL KNOWN that citizens and residents of the United States have a wide variety of rights. The most famous, of course, appear in the Declaration of Independence: the right to life, the right to liberty, and the right to the pursuit of happiness. The meanings of these rights are obvious, but sometimes interpreting them can be confusing.

For instance, your boss compliments you on how good you look in short skirts and suggests that you wear them more often, and your boss is a woman. Is that sex discrimination? How about if she suggests that women your age shouldn't wear short skirts? What if your boss wants you to work in a situation that you have reason to believe is dangerous—can that boss fire you if you refuse? You may be putting up with behavior that you don't have to—behavior that may even be against the law.

RECOGNIZING SEX DISCRIMINATION DOESN'T HAVE TO BE COMPLICATED

Normally sex discrimination occurs in two forms: employment and sexual harassment. The discriminatory practices in employment can occur in the following areas:

- hiring and firing

- compensation, assignment, or classification of employees

- transfer, promotion, layoff, or recall

- job advertisements
- recruitment
- testing
- use of company facilities
- training and apprentice-ship programs
- fringe benefits
- pay, retirement plans, and disability leave
- other terms and condi-tions of employment

UNWELCOME ADVANCES MEAN SEXUAL HARASSMENT

Workplaces often have a friendly atmosphere, but what if that atmosphere becomes "too friendly"? If anyone in a position to af-fect your employment con-fronts you with unwelcome sexual advances, including touching you or requesting sexual favors, that's sexual harassment. The harasser's conduct must be unwel-come to you, and it is help-ful for you to inform the harasser directly that the conduct is "unwelcome and must stop."

The harasser can be your supervisor, an agent of your employer, a supervisor in another area, a coworker, or even a nonemployee like a customer or supplier. Both men and women can be harassers, and both men and women can be victims. In fact, the harasser and victim do not even have to be of the opposite sex. People can be discriminated against by members of their own gender, but typically sex discrimination involves men discriminating against women. Also, the victim doesn't even have to be the person who was actually the target of the harass-ment. Anyone affected in any way by the offensive conduct can be considered a victim.

SEXUAL HARASSMENT WITHOUT THREATS

If a person believes that he or she is forced to work in a "hostile environment," that can also be considered sexual harassment. Because the victim's point of view must be considered, a hostile environment can even include some elements that fit into a stereotyped notion of acceptable behavior. An example of such a situation might be a workplace in which few or no women have worked in the past. If new female employees are exposed to *unwelcomed* sexual pictures of women, sexual slurs, or other offensive conduct, this can be a hostile workplace and can qualify as sexual harassment. Sexual harassment must be considered on a case-by-case basis. The same things do not offend everyone. Those who feel offended have been harassed, while those who do not feel offended have not been. The Equal Employment Opportunity Commission (EEOC) says that a hostile work environment can consist of elements that many people may think are harmless or insignificant. It's this case-by-case basis that often makes charges of harassment confusing.

FOR HELP

Most employers with 15 or more employees are covered by the EEOC's laws, and many smaller employers are covered by state and local laws. For more information, call the EEOC at 800-669-4000. You can also find more information on the EEOC Web site at www.eeoc.gov/facts/fs-sex.html or on the Department of Labor's Women's Bureau Web page, www.dol.gov/dol/wb/public/wb_pubs/sexual.htm.

DON'T BE IN THE "DARK AGES" ABOUT AGE DISCRIMINATION

If you are over 40 and your job opportunities have been limited by unequal pay or lack of equal access to promotions, or if you have lost your job in "downsizing" to be replaced by a younger worker, you may be a victim of age discrimination.

Signs of age discrimination include:

- not being hired because the employer wanted a younger-looking person

- being passed over for training courses and then receiving a negative job evaluation because you weren't "flexible" in taking on new assignments

- being fired or laid off because your boss wanted to keep younger workers who are paid less

- receiving undeserved negative performance evaluations and then having your employer use your "record" of poor performance to justify demotion or termination

- being turned down for a promotion to a middle-management job, which went to someone younger hired from the outside because "the company needs new blood"

WHAT THE LAW SAYS

The Age Discrimination in Employment Act (ADEA) applies to employers who have at least 20 workers (for some reason, employers who have 15-19 workers are governed by most EEOC laws but not by the ADEA). According to the ADEA, employers are *not* allowed to:

- recruit or ask an employment agency to send only young job applicants

- withhold training opportunities for workers

- fire or force a worker to retire because he or she is "over the hill"

- allow younger workers certain benefits, such as flexible schedules, part-time work, job sharing, and telecommuting, while denying such options to workers age 40 and over

You can find more information online at www.eeoc.gov/facts/age.html or, specifically for age discrimination against women, www.dol.gov/dol/wb/public/wb_pubs/age.htm.

IF YOU THINK YOU ARE BEING DISCRIMINATED AGAINST

What can you do if you think you are the victim of discrimination in employment? Here are a few suggestions.

• Write down the date, time, and place of the incident as soon as possible.

• Keep your notes and copies of your job evaluations (as well as any letters or memos that show that you do a good job) at home, not in the office.

• Talk to other workers who may have had trouble at work because of their age or sex. The National Labor Relations Act protects your right to meet together and to try to improve your working conditions. For more information, contact the National Labor Relations Board, 202-273-1991.

• Talk to your employer. If your supervisor is the person doing the discriminating, go to his or her boss, your union, your company's equal-employment officer, and/or the EEOC.

• Don't put off filing a complaint; you have only 180 days in which to file.

If you determine you need to file a charge, you can find more information and assistance at the Web site of the National Labor Relations Board (NLRB), www.nlrb.gov/assist.html, or call the NLRB's Division

THE CIA—A WARM, FUZZY EMPLOYER

In the movies, Central Intelligence agents would kill you as soon as look at you. But in real life, the Central Intelligence Agency (CIA) is one of the most benevolent employers around, especially to its employees with disabilities. The CIA goes to such extremes to hire folks with disabilities that they have become the model for all employers. The agency even has a whole department dedicated to helping people with disabilities become CIA employees.

of Information at 202-273-1991.

IF IT'S TOO DANGEROUS—SAY, *NO!*

Employees have the right to refuse to do a job if they believe in good faith that they will be exposed to an imminent danger. "Good faith" means that even if that imminent danger is not ultimately found to exist, the worker had reasonable grounds to believe that it did exist. The Occupational Safety and Health Administration (OSHA) provides protection to all workers.

You have the right to refuse to do a job, but you do not have the right to walk off the job because of unsafe conditions. If you do that and your employer fires or disciplines you, OSHA may not be able to protect you. Stay on the job until the problem can be resolved. Your right to refuse to do a task is protected if all of the following conditions are met:

- Where possible, you have asked the employer to eliminate the danger, and the employer has failed to do so.

- You refused to work in good faith. Your refusal cannot be a disguised attempt to harass your employer or to disrupt business.

- A reasonable person (or most people) would agree that there is a real danger of death or serious injury.

- There isn't enough time, due to the urgency of the hazard, to get it corrected through regular enforcement channels, such as requesting an OSHA inspection.

When all of these conditions are met, you should take the following steps:

- Ask your employer to correct the hazard.

- Ask your employer for other work.

- Tell your employer that you won't perform the

work unless and until the hazard is corrected.

- Remain at the workplace until ordered to leave by your employer.

If your employer discriminates against you for refusing to perform the dangerous work, contact OSHA immediately. You can't be punished or discriminated against for exercising your rights.

The OSHA Act and other laws protect workers who complain to their employer, union, OSHA, or other government agencies about unsafe or unhealthful conditions in the workplace. You cannot be transferred, denied a raise, have your hours reduced, or be fired as a result of a health-and-safety action. Help is available from OSHA for whistle-blowers. But complaints about discrimination must be filed within 30 days of the alleged reprisal.

The OSHA Web site makes it possible for you to look up the record of any safety inspections of any employer since 1972. You can find that Web site at www. osha.gov/cgi-bin/est/est1.

OSHA ENFORCES

Most OSHA inspections are unannounced (the better to find problems before anyone can hide them). When the inspectors do

WORKPLACE FATALITIES ARE DOWN

Since 1970, workplace fatalities have been reduced by half. Occupational injury and illness rates have been declining for the past six years, dropping in 1998 to the lowest level on record. But there is much more to do. Nearly 50 American workers are injured every minute of the 40-hour workweek, and almost 17 die each day. Federal and state OSHA programs have only about 2,500 inspectors to cover 100 million workers at six million worksites. Workers must play an active role in spotting workplace hazards and asking their employers to correct them.

WORKPLACE SURVEILLANCE MAY INHIBIT PRODUCTIVITY

"Employees who believe they are being secretly surveilled at work are less likely to feel that they have the opportunity to communicate with their peers—even if they need to get information to perform their jobs. They often act as if they are isolated in their own little cells, unable to reach out to even those sitting next to them," reports Purdue University Associate Professor of Communication Carl Botan.

He says employees in situations like these may fear that surveillance will pick up only parts of their conversations, allowing their necessary work communication to be misunderstood. And, it gets worse. Surveillance of this kind is often invisible, so employees don't know if they're being watched or not. Even if they're not secretly being watched, some employees may feel paranoid and suspect that they are. The productivity of those employees will fall to the same level as if they really were being monitored. "Employees who feel they are surveilled are more uncertain about their role in the workplace and seem to have lower self-esteem," Professor Botan says.

show up on a business's doorstep, a member of management and an employee union representative are allowed to accompany them during their inspection. If the business has no union, the employee representative might be from an employee safety committee or can simply be a person chosen for the task by other employees.

If the inspectors find any problems, fines may be as high as $7,000. Willful and repeated violations can have penalties as high as $70,000. These penalties may be discounted if an employer has a small number of employees, has demonstrated good faith, or has few or no previous violations.

If an employer is found guilty of a willful violation that resulted in the death of an employee, that offense is punishable by a court-imposed fine or by imprisonment for up to six months, or both. A fine of up to $250,000 for an individual, or $500,000 for a corporation, may be imposed for a criminal conviction.

OSHA—A POSSIBLE BREATH OF FRESH AIR?

Even without official indoor air standards (see sidebar below), you may still be able to get relief from OSHA. If you're required to work in a place like the smoking section of a restaurant or bar, and if you feel your health is in danger, you may still have some recourse. Section 5(a)(1) of the law that created OSHA requires employers to furnish a place of employment that is free of recognized hazards that are causing or are likely to cause death or serious physical harm to the employees. If a worker needs to enter contaminated air in order to perform some work, OSHA-permissible exposure limits

SMOKE FREE—NOT EXACTLY A GUARANTEE

The official line from OSHA is that they're developing guidelines to regulate indoor air, guidelines they've been working on since 1994. That seems like a long time not to arrive at any conclusions. The official reason they're moving so slowly is that more than 110,000 people have filed written comments or testified during six months of hearings, and processing that many comments takes incredible amounts of time. But that might not be the real reason. An OSHA insider has suggested that OSHA isn't really working on secondhand smoke standards at all. Furthermore, OSHA isn't going to work on those standards as long as they can make the public think that they are.

After they held the secondhand smoke hearings, our insider said, OSHA received 120,000 comments on standards for ergonomics to deal with repetitive motion injury and processed them all in one year. Apparently, OSHA is hoping that if they can draw their "alleged" secondhand smoke decision out long enough, it will go away.

apply to the situation. It doesn't matter how the air became contaminated. However, don't complain if part of that smoke is yours.

NEED HELP FROM OSHA? YOU'RE ON YOUR OWN— SORT OF

All employees are either covered by OSHA, by their own state agencies with equal or higher standards, or by similar health and safety guidelines for federal employees. If you feel you are in a dangerous work situation, you can go to OSHA for help. But you are literally the one who has to do it—not a parent, spouse, or concerned friend, although they can assist you. The name of the person filing the complaint can be kept confidential. OSHA will not tell your employer who filed it. You can file a complaint on OSHA's Web site, www.osha.gov/as/opa/worker, in writing to OSHA, or by telephone call to the nearest OSHA area office. You may also call

the office and speak with an OSHA compliance officer about a hazard, a violation, or the process for filing a complaint. For domestic inquiries, call 202-693-1999; for international inquiries, 202-693-2400.

If you have an emergency and need to report a fatality or imminent life-threatening situation, do not send e-mail. Call OSHA immediately at their toll-free number, 800-321-OSHA (6742).

NEGOTIATING OSHA'S WEB SITE

This may be harder than getting your boss to correct dangerous working conditions. If you are having a hard time finding what you need using OSHA's search engine, go to a search engine that allows you to ask questions in sentences, like www.google.com. Although you may also be directed to private Web sites, ultimately, you're likely to be directed back to the correct OSHA site.

UNDOCUMENTED? YOU'RE STILL PROTECTED

Every worker in the United States is protected by all labor and anti-discrimination laws—even if the worker is in the country illegally. The EEOC believes that if employers were allowed to discriminate against undocumented workers, they would have no motivation to hire U.S. citizens and documented workers.

THE ANSWERS TO THE QUESTIONS AT THE BEGINNING OF THIS CHAPTER

Now that you've read the chapter, it will be much easier to answer the questions from the opening paragraph. Your boss compliments you on how good you look in short skirts and suggests that you wear them more often, and your boss is a woman. Is that sex discrimination? Yes, if she makes you feel that a condition of your employment is dependent on your wearing short skirts. Yes, if her talking about you and your skirts makes you uncomfortable. If she continues after you ask her to stop, she is creating a hostile work environment for you.

How about if she says, "Women your age should not be wearing short skirts"? Is that age discrimination? Yes, if any younger women are allowed to wear short skirts. When young women are allowed to wear short skirts, all women should also be allowed to wear short skirts.

And if your boss wants you to work in what you believe is an unsafe environment? You don't have to do it.

TIPS FOR TRAVELING

★ ★ ★ ★

EVERYBODY LIKES to get away from home every once in a while. Seeing other parts of this country, or even other parts of the world, can be a very enlightening experience. If you're about to make a trip, especially if you're crossing the border into another country, there's a lot of information the government can provide before you go. And there may be a few tidbits you'd like to know before you come home again, as well.

PASSPORTS IN A HURRY

It typically takes six weeks to get a passport using the regular application process through your post office. If you pay $35 extra, you can get "expedited" service that will put a passport in your hands in two weeks. But if you've really got an emergency and need a passport *now,* call your U.S. senator or representative's local office. Those big dogs can move mountains at the State Department when they need to, and it's likely that your member of Congress even has a person assigned specifically to handle such requests for constituents. Makes sense. They'll certainly get *your* vote if they come through with the documents in time, won't they?

THE PENTAGON'S SECRET "SAFE AIRLINES" LIST

It would be handy to know which airlines are safer than others, wouldn't it?

Big Brother Not Only Watches Over You—He Watches Under You

If you drive through a modern tunnel, like the Hanging Lake Tunnel on Interstate 70 in Colorado, the Ted Williams Tunnel in Boston, or the Trans-Koolau Tunnel on Hawaii's Interstate H-3, you pass over electric coils similar to electric magnets. They tell a computer in the tunnel control room the speed and length of your vehicle. If you enter the tunnel but don't cross the next electric coil, an alarm goes off to signal the tunnel operators that you have stalled, had a breakdown, were in an accident, or at least have some sort of problem. The ever-present TV cameras in the tunnel automatically zone in, and the operator starts video-taping. Help will not be far away. On the other hand, if you're driving extremely fast or otherwise acting weird, they can video-tape your entire trip through the tunnel. Like any concerned citizen, they'll call the police to let them know that a dangerous driver is heading their way.

But who would know that? Someone does. It's the Pentagon. But they're only willing to tell you part of what they know.

The Department of Defense charters a lot of planes, and they have tough safety standards for those planes. Before they'll use an air carrier, they inspect the airline, its equipment, and its maintenance records. What they won't release are the names of any airlines that failed their inspections. Not only does the Pentagon not keep a list of the airlines that did not make it, they refuse to provide a reason to the failed airlines explaining why they failed. But the Pentagon will tell you, if you pursue them hard enough, which airlines have passed the tough standards to be on the Department of Transportation's approved list.

The domestic passenger carriers that were on the approved list in 2001 are:

- Alaska Airlines
- America West
- American Airlines
- American Trans Air
- Continental Airlines
- Delta Airlines
- Kitty Hawk International
- Miami Air
- Midwest Express
- North American Airlines
- Northwest Airlines
- Omni Air International
- Reeve Aleutian Airways
- Southwest Airlines
- Spirit Airlines
- Sun Country Airlines
- Sunworld International Airlines
- Tower Air
- Trans World Airlines
- United Airlines
- US Airways
- US Airways Shuttle
- World Airways

The list is available through Air Mobility Command Public Affairs at Scott Air Force Base, Illinois, 618-256-4206.

TOP SECRET

Puerto Rico has the ultimate Valentine's present for you—a free wedding. But what if you're busy on February 14? No problem. You can get married for free on any of the other 364 days of the year in big cities like San Juan, and on most business days in smaller towns. In Puerto Rico, judges are forbidden by law from charging fees for any of their services. That includes weddings. If a judge presides over your ceremony, it won't cost you a cent.

UNLESS YOU SPEND A LOT—CUSTOMS WON'T WIPE YOU OUT

If you buy goods in a foreign country and bring them back to the United States, you may have to pay duty on them. It all depends on how much money you and your family spend.

- Your first $400 worth of merchandise is duty-free.

- On the next $1,000 per person, you'll have to pay 4 percent tax.

- Anything over $1,400 reverts to standard import tax for each individual item, determined by its country of origin, not by where you bought it.

- Duty charges apply to gifts and inheritances as well as purchases.

- You even have to pay duty on repairs made to items you brought with you on your trip. If those repairs were done at no charge, you'll pay duty on the going rate.

One point to remember is that families can pool their purchases. If you're traveling with a family of four, for instance, each family member can bring $400 worth of merchandise into the country without paying duty—together, the family is allowed $1,600. If your purchases add up to $1,000 but the other three members of your family only spent $200 each, you won't have to pay duty. Together you bought $1,600 worth of goods, exactly the amount a family of four is allowed. To avoid hassles, before you travel go online to www.customs.treas.gov/travel/travel.htm, and print out a copy of "Know Before You Go."

DUTY-FREE MAY NOT BE A DEAL

You see them at every international airport and on

every cruise ship. Duty-free shops: They're often a great place not to get great bargains. United States Customs can be very taxing people. They don't care where you bought your souvenirs. If you're traveling with your family, and you have more than $400 worth of goodies for each person, you'll have to pay the customary Customs charges on the balance.

All "duty-free" means is that you don't have to pay the duty taxes from the country where you bought the merchandise. Before you travel outside the country, check out the prices at your local discount or liquor store. You might find better bargains. One thing that is convenient about duty-free shops is that they provide a way to get rid of any foreign money you've got left over before you return home.

TOP SECRET

Tobacco products from Cuba are prohibited unless you actually acquired them in Cuba and are returning directly or indirectly from that country on licensed travel. You may not, for example, bring in Cuban cigars purchased in Canada. Persons returning from Cuba may bring no more than $100 worth of goods into the United States.

DON'T PAY DUTY ON YOUR LAPTOP OR CAMCORDER TWICE

Be able to prove that you already own any big-ticket item before you visit the country it came from. Otherwise you might have to pay duty on it each time you bring it back to the United States. If you take your family camcorder with you to Japan, for instance, the Customs officers may want to charge duty to bring it back into this country unless you can prove that you bought it here before your trip.

To prevent hassles, in addition to airsick pills, pack documents that fully describe the item, such as sales receipts, insurance policies, or jeweler's appraisals. To make things easier, you can register your items with Customs before you depart—including watches, cameras, laptop computers, firearms, CD players, and tape recorders—as long as they have serial numbers or other unique, permanent markings. Take the items to the nearest Customs office, and request a Certificate of Registration (Customs Form 4457). It shows Customs that you owned the merchandise before leaving the United States. Keep the certificate for future trips.

USE SELF-CONTROL INSTEAD OF CRUISE CONTROL

If you find the car of your dreams in Canada, Mexico, or even overseas—love it and leave it unless you know for sure that it was made for the U.S. market. It doesn't even matter if it was originally made here if it wasn't made for this market. Unless you read the phrase "this vehicle meets U.S. specifications"

> ## TOP SECRET
>
> Diamonds are a traveler's best friend—as long as they're just diamonds. You pay no duty on loose stones, but you must pay duty on stones that are set. And there is no duty on fine art, but there is duty on accessory items like picture frames.

on the driver's door frame, don't buy it. You will be able to import it, but you won't be able to license it.

If that phrase does not appear on the car, there is another way you can prove that it meets American safety and emission standards. You can contact the manufacturer with the VIN, and they can give you the answer. But expect them to give you a hard time—carmakers don't want to make it easy for you to go to another country to buy a car.

STOCK UP ON ALL THOSE DISCOUNT MEDICINES

Is the high cost of your medicine making you sick?

Sometimes you can get real deals on the same drugs in other countries. But, as usual, those bargains come wrapped in red tape. Residents of the United States who are carrying prescription drugs are subject to certain additional requirements when entering the United States at international land borders. If a U.S. resident wants to bring in a controlled medication but does not have a prescription for it issued by a practitioner (such as a physician or a dentist) licensed in this country and registered with and authorized by the Drug Enforcement Administration (DEA) to prescribe the medication, the resident may not import more than 50 dosage units of that medication. If the U.S. resident has a prescription (issued by a DEA registrant) for the controlled substance, more than 50 dosage units may be imported, provided all other legal requirements are met.

One more thing. Only medications that can legally be prescribed in the United States may be imported for personal use. The Food and Drug Administration (FDA) prohibits the importation, through the mail or in person, of fraudulent prescription and nonprescription drugs and medical devices. These include unorthodox "cures" for such medical conditions as cancer, AIDS, arthritis, or multiple sclerosis. Although such drugs or devices may be legal elsewhere, if the FDA has not approved them for use in the United States, they may not legally enter the country. If found by Customs agents, these drugs or devices will be confiscated, even if they were obtained under a foreign physician's prescription. For specifics about importing controlled substances, call 202-307-2414.

New Tax Laws and Loopholes

★ ★ ★ ★

THERE MAY BE one thing that's even more inevitable than death and taxes—complicated changes in the new tax law. But these changes can be less complicated and even save you some money, if you know where to look. Here are some tips.

THE 2001 TAX LAW IN ENGLISH

Even though your children have always been priceless to you, their value as a tax credit is going up. This tax credit, worth $500 per child (under age 17 at the end of the tax year) in 2000, will increase to $600 a year from 2001 through 2004. From 2005 to 2008 you'll be able to give your kids credit (at least a tax credit) for saving you $700 a year, and then $100 more for 2009. But according to the tax bill passed in 2001, 2010 will be a banner year for parents. Each child will be worth $1000 off parents' taxes. But enjoy your kids while they're young. In 2011 they'll lose half their value and return to the 2001 level of a $500 tax credit.

A MEDICAL MIRACLE—YOU CAN DEDUCT THE COST OF TRAVELING TO HEALTH CARE

When the medical care you need isn't right around the corner, medical tax deductions for any necessary travel are. They can include:

- bus, taxi, train, or plane fares

- ambulance service

- transportation expenses of a parent who must accompany a child needing medical care

• transportation expenses for a nurse or other caregiver who can give injections, medications, or other treatment required by a patient who is unable to travel alone

• transportation expenses for regular visits to see a mentally ill dependent, if the visits are recommended as a part of the dependent's treatment

You can also deduct out-of-pocket expenses for your car, such as gas and oil, when you use it for medical reasons. You can also include parking fees and tolls. You can't, however, include depreciation, insurance, general repair, or maintenance expenses in your deductions. If you do not want to use your actual expenses, you can deduct a standard rate of 10 cents a mile for use of your car for medical reasons. The cost of fees and tolls can be added to your medical expenses whether you use your actual expenses or the standard mileage rate.

WRITE OFF PART OF YOUR STAY WHILE YOU'RE AWAY

You can include the cost of meals and lodging at a hospital or similar institution in your medical expenses if your main reason for being there is to receive medical care. Under some circumstances, you can deduct the cost of lodging that is not provided by a hospital or similar institution. To deduct those expenses, you must meet all of the following requirements:

• The lodging is primarily for and essential to medical care.

• The medical care is provided by a doctor in a licensed hospital or in a medical-care facility related to, or the equivalent of, a licensed hospital.

• The lodging is not lavish or extravagant under the circumstances.

- There is no significant element of personal pleasure, recreation, or vacation in the travel away from home.

The amount you include in medical expenses for lodging cannot be more than $50 a night for each person. Lodging is included for a person accompanying the patient who meets the qualifications explained above. An example might be a parent who is traveling with a sick child. The parent and child could deduct up to $100 per night for lodging as a medical expense. If you are not in a hospital or similar establishment, your meals are not deductible.

SAVE A LITTLE AND LEARN A LOT

In the medical expenses you're deducting, you can include amounts you've paid for admission and transportation to a medical conference, if that conference concerns the chronic illness of you, your spouse, or your dependent. These costs must be primarily for and necessary to your medical care (or that of your spouse or dependent). Also, the majority of your time during the conference must be spent attending sessions on medical information—there's no leeway for sightseeing instead. And eat well before you go. Your costs for meals and lodging while you're at the conference are not deductible.

WHAT YOU CAN'T DEDUCT AS A MEDICAL EXPENSE

The doctor says, "What you really need are two weeks in Florida." And the doc may just be right. A little golf and a lot of sunshine may be just the ticket for you to return to better health. Unfortunately, your ticket to get there and any other expenses will not qualify as medical deductions on your taxes. Those spoilsports at the IRS say a trip or vacation taken merely for a change of environment, improvement of morale, or general improvement of health—even if you make the trip on the advice of your doctor—is fiscal bad medicine.

You're also not allowed to deduct transportation expenses if, for nonmedical reasons only, you choose to travel to another city for an operation or other medical care prescribed by your doctor. If you can get the same medical care at home, you're on your own if you decide to go somewhere more pleasant to receive your care.

THE IRS WILL HELP YOU STOP SMOKING

You can include in your medical-expense deductions any amounts you pay for a program to stop smoking. If you paid for a stop-smoking program in 1997 or 1998, you may be able to file an amended return on Form 1040X to add those expenses into your deductions for those years. What the IRS won't allow, however, are deductions for nonprescription drugs, such as nicotine gum or patches, that are designed to help you stop smoking.

ADOPTING CHILDREN JUST BECAME LESS EXPENSIVE

Tax credits for expenses associated with adopting children have been increased. Under the new tax law, if your family income is below $150,000 a year, you can receive a tax credit of up to $10,000 for these expenses. That credit will increase with inflation after 2002. If your new family member is a child with special needs, beginning in 2003 you will qualify for a $10,000 tax credit, regardless of how much the actual adoption expenses were. For more information on the adoption tax credit, call 800-829-1040.

REMOVING LEAD-BASED PAINT CAN REMOVE SOME TAX LIABILITIES

If there is a child in your home who has or has had lead poisoning from eating lead-based paint, you can deduct the cost of removing lead-based paints from surfaces in your home as a medical expense. These surfaces must be in poor repair (peeling or cracking) or within the child's reach. Unfortunately, you can't deduct the cost of repainting after the original paint has been scraped and removed.

If, instead of removing the paint, you cover the area with wallboard or paneling, you'll have to treat these items as capital expenses rather than medical deductions.

Marriage Penalty Relief

There is nothing in IRS regulations called a marriage penalty—but in the new law there is plenty of marriage penalty relief.

Beginning in 2005, the standard deduction for married couples filing joint tax returns will be worth 174 percent of the deduction for a single taxpayer. By 2009, a couple's standard deduction will be the same as two single folks. If you're married and in the 15-percent tax bracket, you get larger savings even more quickly. Your standard deduction in 2005 will be 180 percent of what a single person would pay. Your tax credit tops off at 200 percent a year earlier than the rest, 2008. Unfortunately, that new credit disappears completely in 2009. Couples with higher incomes will also benefit, but by a smaller percentage.

Giving Away Money Is Getting Cheaper

When you pass on to the Great Tax Shelter in the Sky, you may not worry much about the taxes your estate will have to pay, but your heirs sure will. With the new law, they won't have to pay as much out of your estate, which means they'll get to inherit that much more. Beginning in 2002, the amount of money exempt from estate taxes will go up to $1 million. By 2009, estates valued up to $3.5 million will be tax free—but only for one year. In 2011, like all changes in the new tax law, estate taxes will revert back to the 2000 level. But even before then your estate won't save quite as much as it may appear to. The tax credits for estate taxes provided by each state will be reduced by 25 percent in 2002, 50 percent in 2003, 75 percent in 2004, then be repealed altogether in 2005. What that means is that up to now, your state government has given a tax credit for any estate taxes paid to the federal government. By 2005, that credit will disappear—some of the money you save on your federal taxes will be owed to your state taxes.

GIFT TAXES GOING DOWN

Gift taxes, the tax paid by the giver on the amount of gifts to an individual that go beyond $10,000 ($20,000 for a married couple), will be reduced. In 2003, the maximum tax rate will be 49 percent of the gift, and that will drop to 35 percent in 2010 and then disappear completely in 2011. In the past there has been no gift tax on gifts that are used for college tuition (if the money is paid directly to the educational institution), medical expenses, and gifts to charities and political parties. That policy will continue. There is also no tax on any size gift that's given to a spouse.

YOU CAN ADD MORE TO YOUR IRA

In past years, you have not been allowed to invest more than an annual amount of $2,000 to your Individual Retirement Account (IRA). That number's going up! Beginning in 2002, you will be able to add $3,000 to your IRA, and up to $5,000 by 2008. After that, this amount may still go higher after it's possibly adjusted for inflation in 2009. If you're already close to retirement—over 50—your IRA contributions can be slightly higher. Depending on the year, you'll be able to invest $500 or $1,000 more in your IRA than younger investors.

QUICKER VESTING MAKES PENSION PLANS BETTER INVESTMENTS

Being "vested" means that if you leave a job where you've invested in your employer's pension plan, you are eligible to take the share your employer contributed as well as your own contributions. In the past, it has taken five years to become vested, but beginning in 2002, you can be-come completely vested in your employer's pension plan in three years or become 20% vested each year from 2 to 6 years of service (instead of 3 to 7 years, the previous amount of time needed).

YOU CAN TAKE IT WITH YOU

Beginning in 2002 you will be allowed to roll over 401(k), 403(b), 457, and IRA retirement plans. That means when you change employers you can take your retirement plan with you to your new employer rather than being forced to

HOW YOUR TAX DOLLARS ARE MISSPENT

The General Accounting Office (GAO) is the watchdog of the federal government and its agencies. Officials there want to know if you've seen any waste, abuse, or mismanagement of federal funds. If you are aware of any problems of that sort, here's how you can contact them:

• via e-mail at fraudnet@gao.gov

• by fax at 202-512-3086

• by mail at GAO Fraudnet, 441 G Street NW, Washington, D.C. 20548

You can also read about waste the GAO has uncovered. Take a look at www.gao.gov or your nearest Government Publishing Office bookstore to find GAO publications.

cash out. However, the new employer's plans are not required to accept rollovers from other plans, so negotiate the ability to roll over your retirement plan as a condition of employment with your new employer.

YOU DON'T NEED A COMPUTER TO FILE ELECTRONICALLY

Use your phone line if you're not online, and receive many of the same benefits as moving your money through your modem:

- Faster refunds: Taxpayers who e-file get their refunds in less than half the time of those who file paper returns, even faster with Direct Deposit.

- More accurate returns: E-filed returns are more accurate and reduce your chance of getting an error letter from the IRS.

- Quick electronic confirmation: Computer e-filers receive an acknowledgment that the IRS has received their returns. Callers using TeleFile receive a confirmation number while they're still on the phone, letting them know that the TeleFile system has accepted the filing of their return.

- No paper: If you use your computer, you can even sign online with a special electronic signature. John Hancock, eat your heart out.

POSTAGE PLUS

★ ★ ★ ★

IT ISN'T your father's post office any more. The U.S. Postal Service has more retail stores than any business in the world, and it hires more employees than any employer other than Wal-Mart. In fact, for the majority of Americans, this is the most frequent contact they have with the federal government. But the post office just keeps adding new and improved features. In fact, it can now be a source of ready cash, even as it leads in developing new technology to eliminate cash.

MAIL IT HOME INSTEAD OF SHIPPING IT

If you bought more than you can carry home on your international trip, don't mail your new purchases home—mail your dirty laundry, instead. You'll save money at Customs.

Write "American goods returned" on the outside of the package. You can even write "dirty laundry," if you want to. Your package may be opened, though, and if it contains anything that is new or not declared—anything that doesn't qualify as "American goods returned," you'll be charged a customs fee for everything in the package.

But, and this is very important, since this is the U.S. Postal Service chapter, we're talking about mailing, not shipping. International shipping and mailing are very different. Shipping, no matter what the packages contain, will have to clear Customs. Also, when you ship, a courier will charge you not only the costs of duty and handling, but also a brokerage fee for clearing the goods through Customs. That fee can be expensive, because it's based on the time and work involved by the brokerage firm rather than the value of the package.

TOO MANY PACKAGES AT ONCE

There can't be any such thing as too many packages, can there? Yes, there can. If you have friends and relatives overseas who will be sending a lot of presents all at once at holiday time or for a wedding or birthday, it really will pay to arrange in advance when the packages arrive. Uncle Sam will help you celebrate, but he's really picky about how he helps.

Customs will waive any import duties on any package worth less than $100—but for only one package each day. If two or more gifts arrive in your mail on the same day, you'll have to pay duty on all of them.

But sometimes good old Uncle Sam is willing to give you a better break in mailing from other countries. For instance, he'll waive the duty for goods worth up to $200 when you mail them to yourself when you're overseas. But the same one-package-per-day rule applies.

IT'S OFFICIAL—CASH IS OUT OF STYLE

The world's largest retailer doesn't want cash anymore. Postal Service research says cash is the most expensive way to handle money at its more than 38,000 retail outlets.

It costs them about 4.8 cents per dollar to process old-fashioned real money. Checks cost 4 cents, credit cards cost 2.7 cents, and debit cards cost only 1.5 cents per dollar processed.

Need Cash When You're Not Near a Fee-Free ATM? Go to the Post Office

The post office doesn't like cash, not only because of the high cost of handling it, but also because it can be stolen. But their solution can be handy for you. They will give customers up to $50 over the amount of a purchase when customers pay with a debit card. You can buy as little as one stamp, pay with your debit card, and get cash back.

This great deal isn't available on demand—only when that particular post office has more cash on hand than they need. Sometimes they may not be able to help you out until a few hours after the post office opens.

The reason cash is so expensive is because it has to be handled so many times by so many people at both the post office and the bank, and because it has to be moved in armored cars or armored mail trucks. And it requires incredible amounts of paperwork. On the other hand, with credit cards or debit cards, once the card is swiped, everything that takes place from that point on is electronic.

Competition Can Be Tough—Even the Post Office Uses FedEx

Congress has prohibited the postal service from giving volume discounts and having private contracts with businesses. As a result, federal agencies, including the Postal Service, can do volume overnight shipping for less through outside contractors like FedEx—just like private companies can.

But, there's more. U.S. mail is also sometimes moved on FedEx airplanes. Even though FedEx only carries packages, it's one of the largest airlines in the world. Through a $6.3 billion, seven-year agreement the Postal Service has with FedEx, the overnight shipper will provide 443,000 cubic feet of transportation space by day and will carry 250,000 pounds of cargo at night, moving Express Mail, Priority Mail, first-class mail, and some international mail. Under the contract, FedEx will also be allowed to put its collection boxes on post office property. After a trial period, other nationwide carriers will have the same opportunity.

PAY YOUR BILLS WITHOUT USING THE MAIL

This is what the Postal Service hopes will happen with their new U.S. Postal Service's eBillPay™. This program lets you schedule and make various payments, as well as receive and pay bills, all online.

- Your money is automatically withdrawn from your checking account.

- You can pay anyone, anytime, anywhere in the United States.

- You can also set up repeating payments, such as a car payment or rent.

- If the payee doesn't accept electronic checks, the postal service will mail a paper one.

- You can schedule single payments up to a year in advance.

The only payments you cannot make through this bill-payment service are court-ordered payments and state and federal tax payments.

The cost for this service is either $6 per month for 20 payments and 40 cents

TOP SECRET

Whatever happened to Mr. Zip? He was a blatant victim of age discrimination—summarily fired and replaced by a younger technology.

Actually, the cartoon character was based on zip codes. Now, however, instead of zip codes, the postal service is into bar codes, electronic messaging, the use of the Internet, and the world's most sophisticated optical character recognition programs to read handwriting.

each for additional payments, or $2 per month and 40 cents per payment. Postal officials say their new service is especially convenient for people who travel frequently. They can keep their bills paid and up-to-date from their laptop computer.

GREETING CARDS MAILED FROM YOUR COMPUTER

Need to send a greeting card? You only have to go as far as your computer with the Postal Service's NetPost CardStore at www.usps.com/netpost/cardstore. This Web site allows you to create cards in your computer, have them printed out in hard copy, and then mailed directly to the person and address—or the people and addresses—of your choice.

The advantages:

- Your friends will get real hard-copy greeting cards.

- The CardStore has a selection of more than 2,000 custom images to choose from.

- You have the ability to include your own personal photos or other artwork in your card.

- You can send cards with personalized greetings to individuals or to large numbers of people.

- The cost is only $1.35–$3 per card, based on the quantity, design, and postage. That cost includes custom personalization, printing, and mailing services.

MAKING IT COUNT: VOTING RIGHTS AND WRONGS

★ ★ ★ ★

THE UNITED STATES is among the most democratic countries in the world. Political choices are made in the privacy of the voting booth rather than at the point of a gun. Love government or hate it, your vote can change what happens in Washington, D.C. Sure, there's a lot that needs fixing. Problems with voting procedures became all too clear in the 2000 presidential election. And the campaign donations of wealthy people and corporations give them too much influence over our laws. But you can have more influence over government than you might think. Read on.

YOUR DUTIES AS A VOTER

Voting does make a difference. As we saw in the 2000 presidential election, a few votes one way or the other can sway a country. Voters can make sure they'll be able to exercise their right to vote by:

- changing their voter registration when they move

- making sure they are properly registered before each election

- knowing where to vote

- taking identification to the polling place

How Many Ways to Elect a President?

In most states, local or county governments set the rules for elections. That means that voters face an incredible variety of voting methods, depending on where they live.

- In New York City, voters press levers on 50-year-old machines. No one makes spare parts for these machines any more, so workers spend all election day fixing them with parts cannibalized from other machines. Almost 18 percent of Americans vote on lever machines.

- One-third of Americans vote on punch cards. In use since the 1960s, these are counted by mainframe computers.

- Some voters use touch-screen monitors to record their preferences, but these can be confusing and slow.

- Others use paper ballots that must be counted by hand.

- A growing minority of Americans vote using optical scanners that count votes from a form similar to a standardized achievement test. These ballots can be checked for mistakes before the voter leaves the booth.

Voting laws and regulations are administered by each individual state, so they can vary from place to place. If you are not registered to vote, some states allow you to register by mail. In other states, you can register when you renew your driver's license. (One state, North Dakota, does not require voters to register before casting their ballots.) The national mail-in form is at the Federal Election Commission's Web site, www.fec.gov/votregis/vr.htm. Eligibility requirements for each state are listed at www.fec.gov/pages/Voteinst.htm. You can also call your county election board for instructions on how to register.

The Rules for Absentee Ballots

As with other voting regulations, the rules for absentee voting are set by state, county, and/or local officials. So there are no hard-and-fast rules across the board. But here are some typical regulations that absentee balloters face:

- Before you vote by absentee ballot, you must be registered to vote.

- Requests for an absentee ballot must be filled out in advance and witnessed.

- There must be a reason for you to vote absentee.

- Ballots must be postmarked no later than election day.

- Absentee ballot must be signed by the voter.

- You cannot vote in person if you've mailed in a ballot.

Absentee voting is convenient—and much better for the country than not voting at all. Contact your local, county, or state voting officials for more information about it.

YOU CAN SHAPE LAWS

In Congress, most of the real work gets done in committees and subcommittees. By the time a bill reaches the floor of either the Senate or the House of Representatives, its major features are already in place. Amendments submitted by members of Congress can polish it—and it can still be defeated in either house of Congress or vetoed by the president—but if you want a say in our laws, you have to start well before Congress votes on them.

NATIONAL VOTING REFORM—IS IT NEEDED?

Studies have shown that between four and six million votes were not counted in the 2000 presidential election. The causes? Faulty equipment, mismarked ballots, polling place mistakes, and foul-ups with registration or absentee ballots. Possible solutions include getting rid of punch cards and lever machines, reducing "convenience" absentee voting, and training both voters and election officials.

National voting standards would set rules for local and state governments to follow. They could also standardize ballots, eliminating the possibility of another "butterfly ballot" snafu. The problem is that all of this will cost hundreds of millions of dollars. It looks like our government will have to decide how much counting every vote is worth.

This is, of course, what lobbyists do. They try to influence legislators to draft bills favoring their causes. In many cases, lobbyists even draft bills for the legislators. Thankfully, the First Amendment to the Constitution also gives citizens the right to transmit legislative proposals directly to their members of Congress. In practice, because few individual citizens have experience in writing bills, these proposals often come from activist groups. Your state legislature may also propose ideas or legislation for Congress to enact. And, of course, the president can always ask Congress to help him fulfill his campaign promises. Once bills are written and introduced, they are debated and amended in committee meetings. Committees may also request testimony at a public hearing from experts and the public. You can find out more details about how the process works online at thomas.loc.gov (named for Thomas Jefferson). At that Web site, select either "House" or "Senate" from "The Legislative Process" menu.

LOBBY FOR YOUR CAUSE

Yes, you can affect the bills that Congress votes on. But, like the professional lobbyists, it's important to make your case before a proposed law goes to the full House or Senate for a final vote. You've got to make your views known as bills are being shaped in committees. To follow any bills that you think are important, you only need to use the search function at thomas.loc.gov. You can search by word, phrase, or legislator name for the discussions that most interest you. While at this Web site, you can also examine the hearing schedule for any committee to find out when your issue will be discussed. If you prefer to call instead, the House and Senate operator at 202-224-3121 can direct you to the committee office overseeing the issue that concerns you.

Once you've found out when your issue is scheduled to be discussed, you should send a letter briefly outlining your position to each member of the committee—and be sure to specify the bill number so they know what you're talking about. Include any memorable statistics or dramatic personal stories you may have, as well as specific suggestions for modifying the bill or bills under consideration. The more you clarify your issue in the minds of legislators, the more likely the law will be modified in the way you desire.

In addition, form or join a group of like-minded citizens to send a flurry of personal letters and e-mails, or join an advocacy group on your issue. Senators and representatives respond more positively to personal letters than to mass mailings or form letters. It doesn't hurt to have donated huge sums to their campaigns, either, but citizens can still affect outcomes if they are loud and persistent.

TESTIFY BEFORE CONGRESS

The chairman of each congressional committee, who is almost always a member of the majority party, decides who will testify before the committee if a public hearing is called. However, the minority party may also call one or more witnesses.

You may be given your day in Congress—and your odds improve if you've got a particularly moving personal experience relevant to an issue. Experts are also sought to testify. Here are some ways you can get your story out:

- Begin by telling your story to your member of Congress or a congressional aide. Be sure to mention where you live, to prove you're the legislator's constituent.

- Write a letter to the chair of the committee or the ranking member of the minority party on the committee.

TOP SECRET

To learn the outcome of voting on a bill or status of a bill that is still pending, call the Office of Legislative Information on Capitol Hill at (202) 225-1772.

- Contact interest groups in Washington that care about your issue.

- Don't forget that subcommittees also hold hearings and may be more willing to hear you than the full committee.

- Ask if you can insert written testimony into the record if you can't testify.

WHO GIVES? WHO GETS?

Money talks in Washington, we all know that. So it's vital to know who's talking to your senators, your representative, and your president. The Federal Election Commission has kept information on campaign donations for years, but it used to be very difficult to access. Now with the Internet, all of that information is easier to get hold of. The Center for Responsive Politics has made it all available at www.opensecrets.org. (Isn't that an appropriate name?)

Who gives? Where does all the money in politics come from? The opensecrets.org Web site lets you search by industry category, by political action committee (PAC), by soft money donor, or by lobbyist. Perhaps the most revealing function is the "Donor Lookup," a page that allows you to find out whether companies you work for or buy from have donated to federal campaigns or parties—and if they have, how much.

Who gets? Here's where it starts getting really interesting. Who *is* getting all those campaign donations? You can search in a number of ways at the Web site opensecrets.org: by senators' or representatives' names, by congressional committee, by political party, or by congressional race. Here you'll find the top donors and a breakdown of where donations come from on the political spectrum. It can be truly fascinating (or frightening, depending on your point of view) to watch how closely legislation tends to reflect the wishes of big donors.

WHAT'S UP WITH SOFT MONEY?

After the Watergate scandal in 1974, Congress severely limited the amount of "hard money" that could be given to candidates. The term "hard money" refers to money that goes specifically to one particular candidate. Individuals can donate no more than $1,000 per candidate per year. Even more significantly, political parties can donate no more than $22,500 for any particular Senate candidate, and even less for a race for the House. Yet the average winner of a Senate seat spends more than $5 million to get elected, and successfully running for a House seat can cost nearly $1 million. So who makes up the difference?

That's where "soft money" comes in. Soft money provides a way for big-money donors to get around campaign finance limits—these donations are essentially unlimited. Many of them are even untraceable. What are some examples of soft money?

- Unlimited campaign contributions to political parties at the national level can be donated for generic "party-building" activities.

- Joint fund-raising committees raise both limited hard money for candidates and unlimited soft money for parties. The soft money can be spent on any race the political party chooses.

- "Issue ads" may be produced and purchased by any interest group, at any cost. They can criticize a candidate's position on an issue, although they can't specifically urge you to vote for any other candidate. The source of funds for issue ads is typically reported only in the annual report of the non-profit group who bought the ad.

The problem with all this is easy to understand. Soft money gives corporations, unions, and wealthy individuals much more influence over elections than the average voter.

THE REAL DEAL WITH CAMPAIGN-FINANCE REFORM

One of the major thrusts of campaign-finance reform is to reduce the influence of soft money. The McCain-Feingold bill, passed by the Senate in 2001, would ban soft money. Among other things, it would also raise the limit on hard money donations by voters to $2,000, prohibit issue ads during the last two months prior to an election, and prohibit television stations from bumping campaign ads in favor of higher-priced commercials. By taking campaign ads out of the competition for television advertising time, this last provision would lower the cost of broadcast ads for candidates.

But despite being passed by the Senate, reform is not likely to happen any time soon. Senator John McCain wants his version of the bill to be debated by the House, in order to minimize changes in the final bill. The House would apparently rather not pass any bill at all because campaign funding would have to change radically under McCain-Feingold.

Read more about campaign finance reform and other important legislative issues at www.opensecrets.org/news. And if you want something to affect the situation one way or the other, write to your senators and representative. Many of them think no one cares about this issue. We should.

WAY-OUT SECRETS

★ ★ ★ ★

KNOWING HOW the government runs some of its operations, do we really trust them to handle scary things like radioactive nuclear waste, threats of alien invasion, and the preservation of our way of life and our planet for future generations? What secrets lurk in the halls of the Pentagon, the CIA, or the Government Accounting Office, and who is covering them up?

MAJESTIC 12 CONSPIRACY REVEALED—SORT OF

This is definitely a conspiracy—but whose? Majestic 12 may (or may not) have been an ultra-top-secret government program to deal with UFOs and extra-terrestrials. There is very little substantial information we know about it; everything is shrouded in mystery and secrecy. Some documents have been made public through the Freedom of Information Act (FOIA), but their authenticity has been questioned. The program is said to have officially begun in 1947, shortly after an incident in Roswell, New Mexico, where a UFO may (or may not) have crashed in the desert. If such a government program did begin then, how long did it last? Did it end? Is it still going on now? Who knows?

So far, no one has been able to pin down the truth—in public, anyway. But ask yourself, why would someone create such a hoax?

What motive could they have? Then ask, why would the government lie to us about a secret organization formed a long time ago to keep the Roswell secrets? It's all so far in the past by now that it's possible the truth will never be known.

One of the files made available through the FOIA in 1991 contains letters, maps, and other documentation about our government recovering the Roswell site wreckage, examining the alien equipment to find out how it worked, studying the dead bodies of the occupants, and covering up information leaks. It also includes similar information about another alien ship that may have come down near the Texas-New Mexico border. All of the pages are marked "bogus" by FBI investigators, but there is no documentation or reasons given for this verdict. And why would the FBI be keeping secret files of secret documents in the first place if they're just "bogus"?

The FBI's failure to justify this pronouncement makes one wonder. Surely there are many simple ways to prove these documents false, if that's what they are. One of the documents claims to be President Harry Truman's order to his secretary of defense to create "Operation Majestic 12." What about verifying President Truman's signature, for instance? Many lines of type in the document are blocked out by crudely scrawled black marker, as is customary when some of the information in a document remains top secret. But, the names of the 12 officials who supposedly made up Majestic 12 are clearly visible. What about an investigation into the lives of those men? If the government knows the whole incident to be a hoax, where's the proof? Since counterfeiting methods were not as sophisticated in the 1940s and 1950s, such hoaxes should be easy to expose.

Dr. Edgar Mitchell, Apollo 14 astronaut and the sixth man to walk on the moon, is convinced that it's all true—Roswell, Majestic 12, and the rest. He claimed, in an interview on *The Geraldo Rivera Show,* to be aware of still-secret information and to know people who were witnesses to the events.

Here's something to think about. Look at the technology we have—like the Harrier that can hover in one spot then take off vertically, "smart" bombs that displayed our military superiority in the Gulf War and Afghanistan, and now an interspace bomber currently in the development stages. Are we just that smart, or did we have a little bit of secret help?

OUR SECRET PSYCHIC SOLDIERS

During the 1980s, the U.S. Army sent enlisted personnel to a place called the Monroe Institute, located in the rolling hills of Virginia's Blue Ridge Mountains. There they received training in extrasensory perception to be used in military operations. They practiced a technique called "remote viewing," whereby subjects could see, hear, and report on locations by performing out-of-body experiences. They could see what was going on in one location while their body was in another. This handy spy tool was supposed to allow us to view enemies without detection. One method of accomplishing this was to hook up slightly different sound frequencies to each ear, creating a third brain frequency.

In 1995, shortly after the research (as well as its funding by the army) became public, the government announced that the whole experiment had been fruitless—that there was no validity to remote viewing, or psychic spying. In 1998 the whole guidebook, *Defense Intelligence Agency Training Manual for Remote Viewing,* was published on the World Wide Web. You might think that the army's announcement about the failure of these experiments would mean the end of the training facility. You would be wrong. The Monroe Institute continues its work through private funding. The word is that the government never really lost interest, and that secret studies are still being performed. *The Sunday Times* of London even reported that U.S. intelligence had consulted remote viewers to locate Osama bin Laden. More than 80,000 pages of the program's original documents remain highly classified.

CIA USES "WITCHCRAFT" TO DEFEAT OUR ENEMIES

During the Philippine uprising and rebellion of the 1950s, the CIA found a way to strike terror into the hearts of the superstitious population. They would silently capture and kill an enemy soldier, then drill two holes in his neck, drain his blood, and leave the body where it would be discovered. When the body was found by his comrades, the soldiers made the obvious supernatural assumption and abandoned the area immediately.

In certain African involvements, the CIA convinced tribal mercenaries that they could be made impervious to rebel troops by magic spells performed on them. These spells consisted mostly of drinking potions that contained lizards, bats, spiders, and even human bones. Reports are that these methods did not always make their subjects invincible.

While in Vietnam, our military intelligence was informed that the Vietnamese believed the ace of spades to be a death omen. Hoping to gain a psychological advantage, the military planted the cards all over. There was no effect whatsoever to this tactic. Why? It's because the graphics on Vietnamese playing cards are in Chinese symbols. A Vietnamese ace of spades doesn't resemble the ace of spades depicted in Western decks at all.

RADIOACTIVE WASTE SITES

The Department of Energy (DOE) has spent 14 years and $4.5 billion to figure out whether Yucca Mountain in Nevada is dry and stable enough to entomb highly radioactive waste for the next 10,000 years. The site is only 11 miles from the nearest well, and it has been found that the rock in this site is not as dense as previously believed. Since we now know the rock cannot be relied upon to contain a possible leak of radioactive waste, the government is working on a metal containment system to be built into the mountain. But there are more problems.

About five years ago a synthetic isotope of chlorine was found at the site about 1,000 feet below the summit. Well, you may think, it's a site where we plan to store radioactive waste—what's wrong with that? What's wrong is there was no way the isotope should have been there. Created by previous nuclear testing, this isotope arrived at the site by air. Then, carried by water, it seeped down to the 1,000-foot level. If nuclear waste can seep in, why should we believe that it can't seep back out? Scientists on the project, some 1,800 of them, have been confused by this development, and some new methods of sealing the area off may be necessary before we'll have a safe place to contain our nuclear waste.

Another problem being addressed by the Nuclear Regulatory Commission (NRC) is the volcanos that are visible in the area. (They didn't see them until now?) Scientists are in complete disagreement about how old the volcanoes are and the potential hazard they may present.

As all this debate goes on, nuclear waste piles up around the country at sites that may not be stable themselves, waiting for the day the waste can be shipped to Yucca Mountain, which we're learning may not even be big enough in the first place. The site was designed to hold 70,000 metric tons of waste, and already more than that (from nuclear power plants alone) has been stockpiled at various locations. And the military has its own radioactive waste it wanted to place there, too. Another site being considered to take all this overflow is located in Red Wing, Minnesota—adjacent to a casino and a daycare center. Stay tuned.

RECYCLED NUCLEAR WASTE IN BELT BUCKLES, BABY CARRIAGES, AND ZIPPERS

In January 2000, the DOE made a deal with a private company to recycle 126,000 tons of nuclear waste into household products. Fortunately they were stopped—sort of. Since there is no set government standard for this kind of transaction, the deal was limited to only surface-contaminated waste—but there was 121,000 tons of that. Surface-contaminated waste, theoretically, can be cleaned of the radioactive contaminant. The thousands of tons of the waste not included in the deal was eliminated because the radioactive particles were dispersed throughout, like sugar in a cake, and would not be able to be cleaned. This deal was never brought before the public to give the rest of us a chance to comment, but the DOE made $250 million out of it. These materials, radioactive on the outside only, are being sold to manufacturers for use in household products that Americans utilize every day.

TOP SECRET

Here's more proof that Congress often ignores the laws it imposes on the rest of the country. A former recycling coordinator for the House of Representatives once estimated that if only 60 percent of representatives' offices sorted out their office paper for recycling and sold it to a recycling management firm, they could earn the institution $150,000 per year. The word is that they tried it for a while, until they noticed that the house cleaning crew dumped it all in the same bag as the trash. They could have given the cleaning crew new instructions, but they just stopped recycling, instead.